The Shame Instinct

How Financial Shame and Money Avoidance Quietly Take Over

Jordan Ellis

First edition, 2026

Published by Jordan Ellis

Contents

Foreword

I've watched this pattern more times than I can count, and for years I mislabeled it. A friend who runs a business with total command of every line item except the one attached to her own name. A brother who can price out a home renovation to the dollar and still hasn't opened a certain envelope sitting on his counter for going on three weeks. I used to think of this as a discipline problem — like they just hadn't gotten around to the boring adult task of checking a balance. I was wrong, and it took watching the same thing happen at my own kitchen counter to understand why.

There's a specific moment this book is built around: the half-second before you look at a number, where your thumb hesitates over the app, or the mail sits on the counter one more day. I know that moment from the inside, not as an abstraction I researched but as something I've done — closed a tab before it loaded, let a notification sit unread longer than I'd admit to anyone, and called it busyness because busyness is a much more comfortable word than fear.

What changed my mind about what was actually happening wasn't willpower. It was noticing that the dread I felt before looking never matched what I found once I finally did. The number was always smaller and more boring than the story I'd built around it. That gap — between the verdict I braced for and the plain fact waiting on the other side — is the reason this book exists.

Most financial advice is written for people who are already ready to act. It assumes you know your number and just need a better plan for it. This book is for the step before that, the one nobody writes about, because it isn't about spreadsheets or budgets. It's about the flinch. If you've ever closed an app before the balance loaded, or let mail sit unopened because some part of you already knew what it said, this book was written for exactly that moment — and for the version of you that's ready to survive it.

— Jordan Ellis

Introduction

You've read the numbers once. Maybe you closed the tab in the same motion you opened it, the way you'd flinch back from a stove before you even registered heat. Maybe you told yourself you'd "look properly this weekend," and then the weekend came and you found four other things that needed doing first — plausible things, defensible things, things no one could call avoidance. You are not stupid. You are not lazy. You are, right now, one of the most informed, capable people you know about almost everything except the one column of digits that would tell you exactly where you stand. That gap — between how competent you are and how little you know about your own number — is not an accident and it is not a character flaw. It is a system working exactly as designed.

Think about how strange this actually is, stated plainly. You would never let a coworker guess at a project deadline, never let a doctor estimate a diagnosis instead of running the test, never accept "probably around there" as an answer to a question that mattered. In almost every other domain of your life, you're the kind of person who wants the real number — the exact figure, the precise reading, the thing you can actually plan around. And yet here, in the one domain that touches your security, your options, your ability to sleep without a low hum of dread running underneath the night, you've made an exception. You've decided that roughly-knowing is safer than actually-knowing, and you made that decision so quietly, so long ago, that it doesn't feel like a decision at all. It feels like just how you are. It isn't. It's a rule you built, once, under pressure, and have been quietly re-enforcing ever since without ever revisiting whether it still serves you.

This book is about that system. Not about budgeting better, not about a five-step plan to check your balance every morning, not about which account or app or strategy will fix it — this is not financial advice, and you won't find investment recommendations or net-worth targets here. What you'll find instead is an honest account of why looking feels dangerous when the danger isn't really financial at all. The number itself can't hurt you. It's just information. What can hurt you — what genuinely feels threatening at a level below language — is what the number might confirm about who you are. That you're behind. That you've been fooling yourself. That the story you tell about your own competence doesn't survive contact with the evidence. Avoidance isn't about the money. It's about protecting a self you're not ready to revise.

This book sits inside a larger series about the instincts that quietly run your financial life without ever announcing themselves as instincts — the reflexes installed so early, or so gradually, that they've come to feel like personality rather than programming. Shame is one of the loudest of these, and arguably the most disguised, because it rarely presents itself honestly. It shows up wearing other people's clothes: forgetfulness, busyness, "I'm just not a numbers person," a hundred small, plausible excuses that all point away from the actual thing happening underneath. This book exists to pull that disguise off, one recognizable scene at a time, until the mechanism is visible enough that you can finally work with it directly instead of around it.

Consider two people, both of whom would tell you, if you asked, that they're "not good with numbers." The first is a thirty-one-year-old nurse who can calculate a medication dosage under pressure at three in the morning without a second thought, who reads lab values and drug interactions and insurance codes all day, and who nonetheless cannot tell you what's in her retirement account, because the one time she looked, two years ago, the number felt so much smaller than she'd assumed it would be that she closed the tab and has, since then, treated the account like a room in her own house she's quietly agreed not to enter. The second is a forty-four-year-old contractor who runs the math on every job he bids — materials, labor, margin, contingency — with a speed and confidence that makes clients trust him instantly, and who still hasn't opened the manila envelope from the IRS sitting on his passenger seat for eleven days, because some version of him already knows what it says and isn't ready to have that confirmed by an actual document. Neither of these people has a numbers problem. They do arithmetic all day, competently, under real stakes. What they have is a very specific kind of number — the one attached to their own worth — that behaves like no other number in their lives. It doesn't get evaluated. It gets survived.

Notice something both of these people share, beyond the surface-level competence: neither of them experiences their avoidance as a decision. Neither would describe themselves, if asked directly, as "choosing" not to look. It doesn't feel like choice from the inside. It feels like simply not having gotten to it yet, like a task perpetually one rung down the list, crowded out by everything more urgent — except the list never actually gets shorter, and the task never actually rises, because something underneath the list is quietly making sure it never does. That something is what this book is trying to name.

That gap is the subject of this book, and it's worth being precise about what this book is not. It is not a claim that shame is always irrational, or that everyone who avoids their finances is secretly fine and just needs a pep talk. Some people really are behind. Some numbers really are bad, and looking at them really will mean facing a hard, unglamorous stretch of repair. This book doesn't ask you to pretend otherwise. What it asks is narrower and, I think, more useful: that you separate the fact of where you stand from the verdict you've pre-loaded about what that fact means about your character — because those are two different problems, and only one of them is solved by looking away.

Each chapter ahead takes one shape this avoidance wears — the unopened statement, the guessed-at balance, the budget you built once and never looked at again, the debt you know the shape of but not the size — and does the same four things to it. Shows you the scene so you recognize yourself in it, not a stranger's cautionary tale. Names the actual mechanism underneath, honestly, without inventing studies to sound authoritative. Counts the real cost, in money and in something quieter — the version of you that keeps shrinking to avoid a truth that was never as large as the fear made it. And hands you two or three moves you can actually make, this week, that don't require becoming a different person, only a slightly braver one for about four minutes.

It's worth naming, too, why money specifically carries this particular weight, more than almost any other domain of adult life. Money is unusual in how thoroughly it sits at the intersection of the practical and the symbolic. A number in a bank account is, mechanically, just arithmetic — deposits, withdrawals, interest, nothing more mysterious than that. But that same number also functions, in most people's minds, as a rough proxy for a dozen other things that have nothing to do with arithmetic at all: how well you're doing compared to your parents at your age, whether you're a burden or a provider, whether the risks you took paid off or didn't, whether you're the kind of adult you pictured becoming when you were young enough to still be picturing it freely. No other single number in a person's life is asked to carry that much symbolic weight while still, stubbornly, remaining just arithmetic underneath. That mismatch — a number's actual, narrow job versus the sprawling identity work it's been drafted into — is where almost all of this book's territory lives.

Why this order, and why these particular eight shapes? Because shame around money isn't one flat feeling — it's a family of related mechanisms that show up in different rooms of your life, and treating them as interchangeable is part of why so much financial advice fails to land. The shame you feel protecting a self-image at checkout is not the same mechanism as the shame you inherited at your parents' kitchen table, even though both produce the identical physical flinch. The shame that makes you grab a check you can't afford is doing different work than the shame that makes you spend twenty dollars to feel better after a collections call. Each chapter isolates one mechanism cleanly enough that you can recognize it precisely — not "I have money shame," which is too vague to act on, but "this is comparison doing this to me right now," which you can actually interrupt. By the end, you'll have a small, specific vocabulary for a feeling that has mostly operated on you without a name, and a feeling with a name is a feeling you can start to negotiate with.

It's worth being direct about who this book is for and who it isn't, because misapplied, well-intentioned advice can do real harm. This book is for the person whose financial avoidance is driven primarily by shame — by a fear of what a number will confirm about their character, rather than by genuine, structural financial hardship with no available options. If you are in acute crisis — facing eviction, unable to cover essentials, drowning under predatory debt with no clear path forward — you need concrete help before you need a chapter on cognitive reframing, and this book will say so plainly when it matters, rather than pretending a mindset shift substitutes for a real safety net. For most readers, though, the situation is subtler: the actual numbers are manageable, sometimes genuinely fine, and the suffering comes almost entirely from the meaning being assigned to them rather than from the numbers themselves. That's the reader this book is built for, and if that's you, the chapters ahead will feel less like distant theory and more like something you've been quietly living for years without a name for it.

You might wonder, reasonably, whether a book can actually change something this old and this wired-in. I want to be honest about what's realistic here. This book will not make the flinch disappear. Nothing will, probably, not permanently — the flinch is likely older than your relationship with money itself, built from a thousand small moments you don't consciously remember, and it will still show up sometimes even after you've read every page and nodded along with every chapter. What changes, if this book works, is something smaller and more durable: the gap between the flinch and the reaction. Right now, for most people, that gap is close to zero — the flinch and the avoidance happen as a single, unbroken motion, so fast you don't experience them as two separate events. The work ahead is stretching that gap wide enough to fit one question inside it: *is this actually the verdict I'm afraid of, or is it just a number?* That's a small thing to ask for. It is also, in practice, almost the entire difference between a life run by shame and a life that simply includes shame as one weather pattern among many.

A note on how these chapters were built, because it matters for how much weight you should give them. Every scene in this book is a composite — drawn from common, recognizable patterns rather than a single real person's exact history, because the whole point is that these patterns are widespread enough that you'll recognize pieces of your own life inside them, not that any one story happened verbatim to any one person. The psychological mechanisms cited, though, are real, drawn from published research by named researchers, cited honestly rather than invented for effect — you can look up every one of them. That combination is deliberate: fiction can carry emotional truth further than a case study can, but only real science should be allowed to explain why the emotional truth exists in the first place. This book tries to keep those two things — the story and the mechanism — clearly separated, so you always know which kind of claim you're reading.

One more thing before the chapters begin, because it will save you some frustration later: you are going to recognize yourself in more than one of these chapters, possibly all eight. That's not a flaw in the book's structure — it's accurate. Shame doesn't confine itself to a single mechanism per person. You may grab checks like the person in Chapter 6 and also carry a family weather pattern like the person in Chapter 4 and also run comparison math in parking lots like the person in Chapter 5. Most people do more than one of these. The chapters are separated for clarity, not because the mechanisms live in separate people. Read for the ones that land hardest, and don't be surprised if that's more than one.

Here is the thesis this whole book stands on, and you can hold it loosely until the chapters earn it: the numbers you refuse to look at were never really about the numbers — they were about who you'd have to admit you are if you looked. Everything from here is an argument for why that admission is survivable, and usually smaller than the dread that's been guarding the door.

One last practical note before we begin. You don't need to read this book in order, chapter by chapter, cover to cover, though it was written to build that way, each chapter's mechanism laying groundwork for the next. If a particular chapter title stops you cold — if "The Mask That Costs More Than the Debt" or "The Punishment You Assign Yourself" lands like it was written specifically about your Tuesday — start there. The book will still make sense. Shame doesn't wait for a tidy reading order, and neither should the relief of finally seeing your own pattern named on a page.

Let's start with the door itself — the moment right before you look, and what's actually happening in you there.

Chapter 1 — The Story You Never Told Anyone

The bank balance sits there in the app, four digits behind a Face ID scan you almost don't complete. You know roughly what it says before you look — the way you know roughly what a scale will say before you step on it — and that roughness is doing a lot of work. It's the difference between a number and a verdict. As long as you don't look, the number stays a number. The second you look, it becomes a statement about you, and some part of you has known that for years, which is exactly why you haven't looked.

This is the scene almost everyone recognizes and almost no one says out loud: not the moment of financial crisis, but the moment right before checking. Standing in a kitchen with a phone in hand. Opening the banking app and closing it before the screen loads. Letting a paper statement sit unopened on the counter for six days, moving it from pile to pile like it might lose potency by association with junk mail. None of this is about the money yet. It's about what happens in the half-second after the money resolves into a figure — the flinch, the tightening in the chest, the fast mental scramble to explain the number before you've even finished reading it. That flinch is the actual subject of this book. The number is just where it lives.

You can watch this exact scene play out in almost any life, once you know to look for it. A twenty-three-year-old lets three separate notifications from the same app stack up on his lock screen, unopened, over a single weekend, because each one is a small, deferred verdict he isn't ready to receive, and stacking them doesn't feel like avoidance from the inside — it feels like being busy, like the weekend simply got away from him. A sixty-year-old woman keeps a specific drawer in her kitchen — not a junk drawer, a very particular drawer — where unopened mail from one specific institution goes, and goes, and goes, while every other piece of mail in the house gets opened same-day. She'd tell you she just hasn't gotten around to it. She has gotten around to everything else in the house within hours. The drawer isn't clutter. It's a filing system for exactly one kind of fear, sorted with more precision than anything else she owns.

Here's the claim this whole book rests on, so let's state it plainly before we go anywhere else: your bank balance isn't only a measurement. It's evidence. Somewhere along the way, without ever deciding to, you started treating what you have — and don't have — as proof of something about your character. Responsible or reckless. Together or a mess. Someone who has it figured out or someone still faking it. The balance doesn't just tell you how much money exists in an account. It tells you, or feels like it tells you, which one of those people you actually are underneath the version you present at work, at dinner, in the group chat. That's why looking can feel disproportionately heavy for something that is, mechanically, just arithmetic. You're not checking a sum. You're checking a verdict on a version of yourself you've been quietly trying to believe.

Here's a small, useful exercise to try right now, before reading any further, because it will make the rest of the chapter land differently: think of the last time you avoided looking at a financial number. Not the general habit — one specific instance, with a specific date, a specific device in your hand, a specific reason you told yourself for why "now wasn't the time." Hold that memory for a moment. Now ask yourself honestly: what, specifically, were you afraid the number would tell you about yourself? Not about your finances — about you. Write the sentence down if you can, even just in your head. That sentence, whatever it turned out to be, is the actual subject of this book. Everything that follows is an attempt to help you meet it directly instead of managing your whole financial life around avoiding it.

Once you see it this way, a lot of behavior that looks irrational suddenly makes complete sense. Why smart, capable people — people who can read a contract, manage a team, solve genuinely hard problems for a living — go strange and avoidant around their own finances. Why someone will happily discuss their salary, their rent, even their debt in the abstract, but go quiet and stiff the moment the conversation turns to their actual number, right now, today. Why a person can know, factually, that checking an account will take four seconds and change nothing about the balance itself, and still avoid it for a week. None of that is a math problem. It's an identity problem wearing a math costume.

Take a man in his fifties, a small-business owner, the kind of person who can tell you within a few hundred dollars what his monthly overhead runs, who negotiates supplier contracts for a living and does it well. His business checking account, he checks daily — has to, it's operational, it's not optional. But his personal retirement account, the one that isn't tied to anything he has to manage this week, hasn't been opened in three years. Not because he forgot it exists. Because somewhere in year two of not looking, not-looking became its own kind of answer — a way of not having to find out whether the plan he made at forty is actually going to hold up at sixty-five, whether the years he spent reinvesting in the business instead of the retirement account were the right call or a mistake he's not ready to name. The business account gets checked because the business account can't punish him with an identity verdict; it's just operations. The retirement account gets avoided because it's the one number attached to a story about whether his whole approach to adulthood worked. Same man. Same competence. Two completely different relationships to two different columns of digits, and the difference has nothing to do with math.

There's an important asymmetry worth naming before going further: the fear of what you'll find is almost always more elaborate, more catastrophic, and more totalizing than what actually turns out to be true. This isn't optimism or wishful reassurance — it's simply how anticipatory dread tends to behave across nearly every domain it touches, financial or otherwise. Dread is unconstrained by fact, so it expands to fill whatever space uncertainty leaves it, and uncertainty about a bank balance is a remarkably roomy space. The actual number, whatever it turns out to be, is always more specific and more bounded than the shapeless dread that preceded it. That gap between the imagined worst case and the actual case is where almost all of this book's practical value lives.

The mechanism underneath this isn't mysterious, and it isn't a personal failing — it's closer to a smoke detector doing its job a little too well. Psychologists who study self-concept describe something called self-verification: people are strongly motivated not just to feel good about themselves, but to have their existing beliefs about themselves confirmed, even when those beliefs are unflattering. If you already suspect, somewhere under the surface, that you're "bad with money" or "always behind" or "not someone who gets ahead," then checking the number isn't a neutral fact-finding mission. It's a test that might confirm the worst thing you already believe about yourself. Avoidance isn't laziness in that moment. It's a defense — an attempt to protect a fragile self-image from evidence that might collapse it. Related research on avoidant coping shows the same shape in other domains: people delay opening medical results, skip the scale, leave the email unread, not because they don't care, but because they care so much that not-knowing feels safer than knowing. The uncertainty is uncomfortable. But it's a comfortable kind of uncomfortable, because it leaves the story still open. Looking closes it.

There's a useful test worth applying here, one you can run on any financial fear to check which category it actually belongs to: ask whether the fear is about an action or about a self. "I'm worried I overspent on groceries this month" is a guilt-shaped worry — specific, bounded, pointed at a behavior you could name and change. "I'm worried about what checking will tell me about myself" is a shame-shaped worry, and it's nearly always the second one hiding behind the first, dressed up in more acceptable, more sayable language. Run this test on your own next flinch and you'll usually find the shame-shaped version underneath within a sentence or two.

This is where shame does something distinct from its quieter cousin, guilt, and the difference matters more than it sounds like it should. Guilt says: I did a bad thing. Shame says: I am a bad thing. Guilt points at behavior — you overspent this month — and behavior can be changed next month. Shame points at identity — you are the kind of person who overspends — and identity feels fixed, inherited, almost biological. Money is one of the few areas of life where the two get fused so tightly that most people can't tell them apart anymore. A missed payment isn't experienced as "I missed a payment." It's experienced as "I am someone who can't be trusted with money," full stop, case closed, verdict delivered. Once the number gets read as identity instead of information, avoiding the number stops being about avoiding data. It becomes about avoiding a courtroom you've already privately convicted yourself in.

The distinction matters because it predicts, with real accuracy, what a person will actually do next. Someone processing a financial setback through guilt tends to move toward repair — call the bank, set up a payment plan, adjust the budget, because a specific behavior invites a specific fix. Someone processing the identical setback through shame tends to move away, toward concealment or freeze, because there's no fix for a self, only a slow, painful revision that feels too large to attempt on a Tuesday night with a bill in hand. This is worth sitting with, because most financial advice — the budgeting apps, the five-step plans, the spreadsheets — is built for the guilt version of a problem. It assumes a person who's ready to act on specific behavior. It has almost nothing to offer the person still stuck at the identity layer, still trying to survive a verdict rather than fix a number. That's the gap this book is written to close, and it's a gap most financial advice doesn't even know exists.

The cost of this shows up in two currencies, and only one of them is dollars. The financial cost is real and specific: unopened statements mean missed errors, unnoticed fees quietly compounding, subscriptions nobody remembers agreeing to, an overdraft that could've been caught on day one instead of day twenty. Avoidance doesn't just fail to fix problems — it actively lets small ones grow teeth. But the quieter cost is the one that does more long-term damage, and it's this: every time you look away instead of looking, you confirm the very story you were trying to avoid. You meant to protect the fragile self-image. What you actually did was starve it of any contradicting evidence. The person who never checks the account never gets to discover that the number was better than feared, that a small change actually worked, that they are, in fact, capable of doing this. They just accumulate more silence, and silence gets misread as confirmation. The story doesn't go away when you don't look. It just goes unchallenged.

Think about what an outside observer — someone with none of your history, none of your dread, just a clear view of the facts — would actually see if they watched a year of your financial life from the outside. They wouldn't see a person who's bad with money. They'd see a person managing a chronic, low-grade fear response, which happens to be aimed at a bank account instead of, say, a spider or a stage. The behaviors that look like financial incompetence from the inside are the unopened envelopes, the guessed-at balances, the six-day delay before checking a statement. From a clinical distance, they look exactly like avoidance behavior around any other feared stimulus. Nobody would call a person with a fear of flying "bad at travel." They'd correctly identify a fear that happens to intersect with travel. The same reframe applies here, and it matters, because "I'm bad with money" invites shame and paralysis, while "I have a fear response to financial information" invites the much more solvable question of how fear responses get worked with — which, it turns out, is a well-understood process that has nothing to do with getting smarter at math.

And there's a subtler cost still, harder to name: the low hum of walking around with a part of your own life you've quietly agreed not to think about. People organize entire routines around it — never opening certain apps after 9pm, changing the subject fast when a friend mentions their savings, feeling a private flare of anxiety at a completely ordinary calendar reminder that says "review budget." That's not a money problem anymore. That's a relationship with a piece of your own reality that you've made adversarial. You end up, in a strange way, hiding from yourself, in your own house, using your own phone.

There's a particular kind of exhaustion that comes from maintaining an internal no-fly zone, and it's worth describing precisely because it rarely gets named. It's not the acute exhaustion of a hard day. It's a low, constant background tax — a small percentage of your attention, all day, every day, permanently allocated to steering around a subject rather than through it. You don't experience this as a distinct sensation most of the time. It just feels like being a little more tired than the day warranted, a little more reluctant to open your laptop in the evening, a little more likely to reach for a distraction the moment a quiet fifteen minutes opens up. The avoidance isn't free even when it's working exactly as designed. It's charging you a subscription fee, deducted in small increments of attention and energy, for as long as the no-fly zone stays active.

There's research that gives this specific shape of avoidance a name worth knowing, because naming it makes it easier to catch. The behavioral economists behind the leading research on scarcity describe how a mind under financial strain doesn't just avoid looking. It develops what they call tunneling — an intense, involuntary focus on the most urgent thing directly in front of you, at the cost of almost everything slightly further out. Under real or feared scarcity, the mind isn't choosing to avoid the retirement account or the credit card statement out of laziness. It's allocating its limited attention to whatever feels most immediately survivable — today's grocery run, this week's rent — and the accounts that require calm, unhurried attention simply never make it into the tunnel. The tragedy Mullainathan and Shafir point to is that this narrowing, which feels protective in the moment, actively worsens the exact problem it's trying to manage, because the things being ignored are often the things that would have eased the pressure — the fee that could be waived with one call, the balance transfer that could cut the interest in half. Avoidance under shame and tunneling under scarcity aren't identical mechanisms, but they compound each other beautifully, in the worst sense of the word: shame makes you not want to look, scarcity makes it neurologically harder to look even when you want to, and between the two, the unopened envelope just keeps getting company.

There's a further cost worth naming plainly, because it's the one most people discover last, usually at the worst possible moment: chronic avoidance actively erodes your ability to accurately assess urgency. Someone who checks regularly develops a reliable internal sense of when something actually needs attention now versus when it can wait — a calibrated instrument, built from repeated contact with real numbers. Someone who avoids for years loses access to that instrument entirely. Everything financial starts to register as equally threatening, equally urgent, equally worth avoiding, whether it's a genuinely time-sensitive problem or a routine statement that requires nothing but a glance. This is part of why avoidance so often produces exactly the crisis it was trying to prevent — by the time the avoided thing finally forces its way into view, usually via a collections call or a bounced payment, it arrives with none of the early warning signs that regular contact would have surfaced months earlier.

None of the fixes here are about spreadsheets or apps or systems — that comes later, and it comes easier than you'd think once the deeper thing loosens. Here, the moves are about interrupting the flinch itself, before it turns into another week of avoidance.

First: separate the look from the plan. Tell yourself, explicitly, out loud if you have to, "I am only going to look. I am not deciding anything today." This sounds almost too simple to matter, but it does the real work — it breaks the fused link between seeing the number and being forced to immediately judge or fix it, which is the exact fusion that makes looking feel so dangerous in the first place.

Second — and this is the Move — the next time you feel the flinch, the urge to close the app before it loads, do this instead: open it, read the number once, and say out loud, "That's just information." Not "that's fine," not "that's terrible" — just information. Then close the app and go about your day without deciding anything else. Do this even though it will feel anticlimactic. It's supposed to. The anticlimax is the proof: you predicted a verdict and got a fact instead. That gap, repeated a few times, is what actually retrains the reflex.

Do this three or four times across a couple of weeks and pay attention to something specific: the gap between what you braced for and what you actually got. Most people, doing this exercise honestly for the first time, discover that the number itself is almost boring — smaller than the dread, less final than the dread, missing the dramatic charge the anticipation always promised. That gap is not incidental. It's the entire mechanism of this book compressed into one small, repeatable action. Every time you survive the anticlimax, you're not just gathering information about your balance. You're gathering information about your own capacity to face a hard fact and remain, afterward, exactly the same person you were before — which is the actual belief this whole book is trying to help you build, one boring anticlimax at a time. Keep a tally if it helps — a simple mark on a calendar each time you look and survive it. After the fifth or sixth mark, most people report the anticlimax itself starts to feel almost predictable in advance, which is exactly the outcome this exercise is built to produce.

Third: notice, and name, the difference between what the number says and what you're about to tell yourself it means.

The balance is a fact. "I'm bad with money" is a story you're about to attach to the fact, and it's optional. You can hold the first without signing up for the second.

Fourth: shrink the tunnel on purpose, once a week, at a time you choose rather than a time scarcity chooses for you. Pick one slow, low-pressure window — Sunday morning with coffee, not the frantic ten minutes before bed — and use it to look at exactly one account you've been avoiding, with nothing else competing for your attention. This works against the tunneling mechanism directly: you're giving your attention a scheduled, unhurried appointment with the exact thing scarcity would otherwise crowd out, so it never has to compete with today's more urgent fire.

One final thought before the chapters that follow take this apart mechanism by mechanism: notice that everything in this opening chapter has been building toward a single, quiet reframe. The problem was never that you don't understand money. Most people who avoid their numbers understand money perfectly well in the abstract — could explain compound interest to a stranger, could budget someone else's finances competently in an afternoon. The problem is that your own numbers stopped being neutral information a long time ago and became, instead, a mirror you've been afraid to look into. Every chapter that follows takes that mirror and, piece by piece, turns it back into what it always should have been: a measurement. Not a mirror. A tool, doing exactly the narrow, useful, forgettable job a tool is supposed to do.

Here's the rule to carry into everything that follows: the number was never the thing you were scared of. You were scared of what you'd have to call yourself once you couldn't unsee it — and that fear, not the balance, is the thing actually worth looking at first.

Chapter 2 — The Good-With-Money Person

Why You Protect a Self-Image Instead of a Bank Account

She sees the total before it registers as a number — she sees it as a verdict.

It's a Tuesday, mid-afternoon, the kind of unremarkable errand that fills up most of an ordinary week — a grocery run, nothing special, a cart with the usual rotation plus a few extras she picked up almost without noticing, the way extras accumulate when you're not paying close attention to a running total. She's tired in the specific, low-grade way that comes from a full week rather than any single hard day, and some part of her, unexamined, has decided that today is not a day for close attention to anything, including this.

The card reader hums, waiting. She's standing in a checkout line with a cart that has more in it than she planned, and for half a second her eyes go to the screen where the total will appear. Then a thought arrives, quick and quiet, barely even language: *a person like me wouldn't need to check.* She doesn't examine it.

She doesn't have time to — it moves through her faster than a decision, more like a reflex. Her thumb finds the card. She taps it to the reader while looking slightly up and to the left, at nothing, the way you look when you're being photographed and told not to smile too hard. The receipt prints. She doesn't take it.

The cashier says something ordinary — the total, a receipt offer, a comment about the weather — and she responds appropriately, on autopilot, the social layer of her running smoothly even while a completely different layer underneath has just quietly executed a maneuver she's performed hundreds of times without ever once naming it. From the outside, nothing happened. A woman bought groceries. From the inside, a small, practiced act of self-protection just ran to completion, invisible to everyone in the store, including, in any conscious sense, her.

In the car, she can't tell you what the total was. She could tell you what she bought. She could tell you the cashier's earrings were shaped like shells. She cannot tell you the number, because she made sure not to let it in.

Watch her closely enough, across enough ordinary days, and you'll notice a whole small choreography built around never quite letting a total register — tapping her card before the screen finishes displaying the amount, glancing away at the exact moment a receipt would print, letting a cashier's small talk fill the specific few seconds where the number would otherwise have a chance to land. None of these are conscious strategies. She'd be genuinely surprised, possibly a little defensive, if you pointed them out to her as a pattern. But pattern they are, refined over years into something close to reflex — a full-body choreography built for exactly one purpose, executed so smoothly it no longer registers, even to her, as effort.

This isn't the only place she does this. It's just the most visible one, because it happens in public, under fluorescent light, with a stranger watching. At home, she pays bills the moment they arrive, same day, sometimes same hour — which looks, from the outside, like admirable promptness, and which functions, on the inside, as a way of never having to sit with an open balance long enough to actually study it. Pay it fast enough and you never really have to read it. She's built an entire system of financial behaviors that look like responsibility and function like avoidance, and the system works so well that even she, most days, can't tell the difference between the two.

Notice the specific words that moved through her, faster than she could examine them: *a person like me.* Not "I shouldn't spend this much," which would be a claim about behavior, correctable, ordinary. *A person like me* is a claim about category — an entire class of person she's decided she belongs to, complete with rules about what that category does and doesn't do, checks and doesn't check, needs and doesn't need. The thought wasn't really about this purchase at all. It was a membership test, administered in real time, at a checkout counter, with the stakes felt as though they were about to determine which category she belonged in for the rest of the day.

This is not carelessness. Careless people look and shrug. She is the opposite of careless — she's the one who color-codes her closet, who replies to emails within the hour, who has never once forgotten a birthday. She thinks of herself, correctly, as a responsible person. Which is exactly why she couldn't look.

Looking risked finding out that the total didn't match what a responsible person's total should be, and if it didn't match, she would have to do something with that information: either change how she spends, or change what she calls herself. Not looking kept both options open a little longer.

Notice, too, how selectively this instinct operates in her life, because the selectivity is itself the clue to what's really going on. She has, in the past year, looked closely and without flinching at a medical test result she was genuinely afraid of, at a difficult performance review, at a friendship that needed an honest, uncomfortable conversation to survive. She is not, in general, someone who avoids hard truths. She avoids exactly one hard truth, in exactly one domain, and the narrowness of that avoidance is the tell — a general aversion to discomfort would show up everywhere. A specific, cordoned-off blind spot shows up exactly where a specific, cordoned-off identity is being protected.

Compare her to a coworker of hers, a man who checks every total, out loud, cheerfully, in front of anyone — "oh, sixty-two dollars for that? Worth it" — and who nonetheless carries a revolving credit card balance he's stopped being embarrassed about, because at some point in his twenties he decided debt was just a normal, unremarkable feature of adult life, the way rent is. He isn't hiding from his numbers. He looks at them constantly. What he's not doing is letting them mean anything — the total registers, gets acknowledged, and then gets filed as simply descriptive, disconnected from any story about who he is or ought to be. He isn't protected by ignorance. He's protected by indifference. Both are ways of never quite closing the loop between fact and identity, and both, over years, let a real number drift further from what a person would do if they actually let the number in.

You'd think these two people — the woman guarding a "responsible" self-image, the man who's simply stopped caring — represent opposite failure modes, and in a sense they do. But they share the same missing step: neither of them ever completes the circuit between *seeing a number* and *letting the number update what they do next.* She breaks the circuit by refusing to look. He breaks it by looking without letting it land. Somewhere between those two failure modes is the actual skill this chapter is pointing toward — seeing a number, letting it mean exactly what it means, no more and no less, and then acting on it. Neither avoidance nor indifference gets you there. Only the harder, narrower path in between does.

You've done a version of this. Not necessarily at checkout — maybe it was the banking app you didn't open for a week after a trip you enjoyed too much to want to cost-account. Maybe it was a credit card statement left face-down, literally or otherwise. Maybe it was a subscription you knew was still being charged and let ride because canceling it meant admitting you'd started it and then abandoned it, which felt worse than the six dollars a month. In each case, the move was the same: a fact was approaching, and rather than meet it, you built a small, fast detour around it. The detour felt like nothing. That's what makes it dangerous — it doesn't feel like avoidance. It feels like being busy, or being fine, or simply not being the kind of person who needs to check.

The detour has a specific, recognizable texture once you know to look for it, distinct from ordinary distraction. Ordinary distraction is diffuse — you got pulled toward something else, no particular thing, just the general noise of a full day. The shame-driven detour is precise, almost surgical, aimed with unerring accuracy at the exact moment a specific fact was about to resolve. You don't get distracted from checking your balance in general. You get distracted at 11:58, right as the app was about to finish loading, by a notification, a thought, a sudden urgent need to do something else entirely. The timing gives it away, if you're paying attention. Ordinary distraction doesn't know what it's protecting you from. This kind does.

Twenty-six years old, three months into his first real job, and he has a system he's proud of: every Friday, he transfers a fixed amount into savings before he can spend it, automatic, untouchable. He tells people about it. It's become part of how he introduces himself financially — "I'm pretty disciplined about saving, actually" — said with the specific pride of someone who built a habit from nothing. What he doesn't mention, because he's arranged his own attention so carefully that he mostly doesn't notice it himself, is that the savings transfer is the only number he ever looks at. He has never once checked what the savings account actually adds up to after eight months of transfers, because some part of him is afraid the total will be smaller than eight months of "disciplined" transfers should produce — that a subscription he forgot about, or a slow leak of small withdrawals, has been quietly undoing the thing he's proudest of. So he protects the ritual and avoids the result. The Friday transfer is real. The evidence of what it's actually building is not something he's willing to look at, because if the total disappoints him, the story he tells about himself — *disciplined, on track, handling it* — doesn't just take a hit. It stops being available to him at all.

What's actually happening

There's a name for the gap she just stepped around, and understanding it changes what you think the checkout-line flinch is actually about.

Psychologist E. Tory Higgins described something he called self-discrepancy: the distance between your *actual self* — who you really are, based on what you actually do — and two other selves you carry around as reference points. One is your *ideal self*, the person you hope to become, the version of you attached to your wishes and ambitions. The other is your *ought self*, the person you believe you're supposed to be, the version attached to duty, responsibility, and other people's expectations of you. Higgins's research found that these two kinds of gaps don't feel the same, and they don't produce the same emotion. A gap between who you are and who you *ideally* want to be tends to produce something closer to disappointment or sadness — the ache of a dream not yet met. But a gap between who you are and who you *ought* to be produces something sharper: agitation, anxiety, and — when the gap is about a self-image you've built your identity around — shame.

It's worth sitting with why the ought-self gap specifically produces shame rather than the gentler sadness of the ideal-self gap. An ideal you haven't reached yet is, by definition, aspirational — nobody expects you to already be there, so falling short of it doesn't implicate your basic adequacy, only your progress. An ought you haven't met is different in kind: it's framed, from the start, as a baseline you were already supposed to have cleared, a standard other people are quietly assuming you meet. Falling short of an ought doesn't read as "still working toward something." It reads as "failing at something you should already have handled" — and that specific flavor of failure, the kind attached to a baseline rather than an aspiration, is precisely the flavor that curdles into shame instead of disappointment.

Here is the part that matters for the checkout line: shame isn't really about the act. It's about what the act implies you are. Guilt says *I did a bad thing.* Shame says *I am a bad thing.* Guilt is repairable — you fix the behavior, you make amends, the discomfort lifts. Shame is not repairable in the same way, because it isn't pointed at behavior. It's pointed at identity. And identity doesn't take corrections gracefully. It defends itself.

That's what the thought *a person like me wouldn't need to check* actually is. It isn't a factual claim. It's a defense mechanism dressed up as a fact, deployed in the exact half-second when the discrepancy between her actual spending and her "responsible person" self-image was about to become undeniable. Her brain didn't choose between looking and not looking based on the number. It chose based on which felt safer: the discomfort of an unknown total, or the discomfort of a known one. An unknown total can still be anything. A known total, if it's bad, forces a verdict — and once you've truly seen a fact, you can't file it back under *not yet decided.*

Higgins's original research went further than just naming the discrepancy — it also mapped which situations make the ought-self gap loudest. His work found that the anxiety spikes hardest not in private, alone, but in moments with an implied audience: when someone else's eyes, real or imagined, are on the outcome. That detail matters enormously for the checkout-line scene. She isn't alone with her own numbers there. There's a cashier, a line behind her, the mechanical presence of the card reader itself, waiting. The ought-self gap doesn't just activate because she's spending — it activates because she's spending *in front of someone*, even a stranger she'll never see again, and the presence of any witness at all is enough to sharpen a private discrepancy into a public one. This is worth remembering for the rest of the book: shame around money rarely peaks in solitude. It peaks in the presence, real or imagined, of an audience — which is exactly why so much of what follows involves learning to check your numbers with no one watching at all.

This is why avoidance so often masquerades as competence. The people who most need to not-look are frequently the people who are otherwise the most careful — because they have the most identity riding on the "I'm careful" story, and the most to lose if a number contradicts it. Sloppiness doesn't produce this flinch. Only a self-image worth protecting does.

This also explains a pattern that confuses a lot of well-meaning advice-givers: telling someone in this position "you should just check your accounts more often" almost never works, and often backfires, producing defensiveness instead of change. The advice assumes the barrier is informational — that she simply hasn't been told checking is important. It isn't informational. She knows checking is important; she could recite the advice herself, word for word, to someone else. The barrier is the flinch, and advice aimed at the behavior without addressing the flinch underneath it is aimed at the wrong layer entirely. It's the equivalent of telling someone afraid of flying that planes are statistically very safe. True, and completely beside the point, because the fear was never really about the statistics.

Consider a third version of the same pattern, this time with the polarity flipped entirely. A fifty-two-year-old woman, recently divorced, has spent the two years since her divorce building an identity around financial independence — she says the phrase often, to friends, to her adult children, to herself in the mirror some mornings, "I take care of myself now." She checks her accounts religiously, more than daily, sometimes several times an hour during stressful weeks, refreshing a balance that essentially never changes meaningfully between refreshes. This looks like the opposite of avoidance, and in the narrow sense, it is — she's not hiding from the number. But the checking isn't information-gathering either. It's reassurance-seeking, a compulsive attempt to keep re-confirming a self-image she doesn't yet fully trust, the same way you might touch your pocket forty times to make sure your phone is still there even though you felt it there thirty-nine times already. The self-image being protected is identical in structure to the checkout-line woman's — "I am a person who has this handled" — but the behavior it produces is inverted. One avoids the mirror. The other can't stop looking in it. Both are managing the same fear. Neither is actually relating to the number as just a number.

There's a second layer to this worth naming, because it explains why the twenty-six-year-old's Friday ritual works so well as camouflage. The social psychologist William Swann has spent decades studying self-verification — a companion idea to self-discrepancy — and one of his central findings is that people don't just seek confirmation of positive self-views, they seek confirmation of *whichever* self-view they already hold, even a shaky or unflattering one, because a confirmed self-concept, positive or not, feels more stable and more predictable than an unconfirmed one. This is why the young saver can be simultaneously proud of his Friday ritual and terrified of the account total: the ritual confirms the self-concept he wants ("disciplined"), while the total risks confirming a self-concept he's quietly afraid is also true ("still, underneath it, careless"). Swann's research suggests people will sometimes go out of their way to avoid information that would disconfirm even a story they don't like, simply because an unconfirmed identity —

genuinely not knowing which one you are — is its own kind of intolerable. Better a stable bad story than an unstable open question. That's not a flattering way to describe the impulse, but it's an accurate one, and it's the same engine running under her checkout-line flinch and his unopened savings total both.

What it costs you

The financial cost is the boring part, and it's real: unopened statements don't stop accruing interest, unreviewed totals don't stop compounding, and a habit of paying without reading is a habit that, repeated fifty-two weeks a year, adds up to a meaningfully worse financial position than the version of her that takes four extra seconds at the register. That's worth naming. But it's not the expensive part. Consider what it actually adds up to over a year: fifty-two checkout lines, or their equivalent — statements, invoices, the quiet math of daily life — each one a small opportunity to catch an error, notice a pattern, register that a subscription renewed at a higher price than she signed up for. Miss all fifty-two, and you haven't just missed fifty-two minor facts. You've missed fifty-two chances to update a self-image that's been running on data from years ago.

There's a specific irony worth sitting with here, because it explains why this pattern is so hard to interrupt from the outside: the more competent someone is in general, the more convincing their avoidance looks to everyone around them, including themselves. Nobody watching her tap the card and look away sees a person in crisis. They see a woman handling her life with total ease. The performance is so smooth it fools the performer as much as the audience — which means there's rarely an external prompt to interrupt it. No one intervenes on behalf of someone who looks, from every visible angle, like she has this handled.

There's a longer-horizon version of this cost worth spelling out, because it's the one that eventually shows up as a genuinely large number rather than a diffuse feeling. A person who never fully lets a total register rarely makes active, informed financial decisions — they mostly just continue whatever pattern is already running, because deviating from the pattern would require actually looking closely enough to decide something different is warranted. Continuing the pattern isn't neutral. It means the subscription that crept from nine dollars to nineteen dollars over three years of unannounced price increases keeps running unnoticed. It means the interest rate on a card that could have been renegotiated or transferred keeps compounding at the higher figure, because renegotiating requires an uncomfortable, close look at the actual number first. None of these individually amount to much. Stacked across a decade of not-quite-looking, they amount to a specific, calculable gap between where her finances actually are and where they'd be if she'd simply been willing to read the number as often as she paid it. That gap has a dollar figure. It's just one she'll never see, because seeing it would require the exact behavior that's been avoided the whole time.

The expensive part is what happens to her relationship with her own life when she can't trust her own read of it. Somewhere underneath the practiced calm, she knows she's been avoiding the total. Not consciously — she wouldn't phrase it that way if you asked her — but there's a low hum of something unresolved that she carries from the parking lot into the rest of her day. It shows up as a vague dread whenever anyone mentions budgeting, a flinch when a friend mentions their own numbers so casually it seems unbelievable, a private worry that everyone else has this figured out in a way she doesn't. She has built a self-image of competence, and she is now spending real energy every day guarding the one part of her life that isn't allowed to test it. That's not being responsible. That's running a small, permanent security detail around a fact.

And the identity cost compounds the way debt does. Every time she looks away instead of looking, the "responsible person" story gets a little more fragile, because it's no longer built on evidence — it's built on the absence of evidence. A self-image that depends on not looking is not a self-image, it's a hope with better posture. She isn't protecting her competence. She's protecting her *belief* in her competence, which is a much smaller, much more anxious thing to guard.

The overrides

Before the overrides, one more thing worth sitting with — a question that tends to surface once you start noticing the checkout-line pattern in yourself: if the flinch is protecting a self-image, whose self-image is it, really? Ask yourself honestly where "a responsible person wouldn't need to check" came from. For most people, tracing that sentence backward leads somewhere specific — a parent who prized discipline above almost everything else, a teacher who praised competence and went quiet around struggle, an older sibling whose approval always came with conditions attached. The self-image being guarded so carefully at the register usually isn't even fully yours. It's an inherited standard, absorbed early, that you've been defending on autopilot ever since, without ever once auditing whether it's a standard you'd choose for yourself if you were building it from scratch today. That's worth knowing before you try to change your relationship to it: you're not just negotiating with your own perfectionism. You're negotiating with someone else's voice, wearing your face.

Name the flinch out loud, the moment it happens. Do this even in public, even under your breath, even if it feels strange the first time — the naming works whether or not anyone else hears it, because the audience that matters is the part of you running the avoidance, not anyone standing nearby. The next time you feel the urge to look away — from a total, a balance, an app icon you're avoiding tapping — say the actual sentence in your head instead of letting it stay pre-verbal: *I'm about to avoid this because of what it might mean about me, not because of what it costs.* Putting language on the reflex slows it down enough to make it a choice instead of a reflex. This alone won't fix your finances. It will fix the part where you don't know you're avoiding.

Separate the number from the noun before you look. Before you check any balance or total, say to yourself: *whatever this says, it is a fact about a transaction, not a fact about my character.* Write it if you need to — on your phone's notes app, once, as a standing reminder. This is the line to text a friend: *the number is a fact, not a verdict.* It sounds almost too simple to matter, but the entire flinch depends on collapsing those two things into one. Pulling them back apart is most of the work.

The Move: look at one number today, on purpose, before you're forced to. Not a full reckoning, not a budget overhaul — one number. Open one statement, one app, one total you've been letting sit unread, and read it fully, today, before the day ends. Don't act on it yet. Don't fix anything yet. Just look, and notice that you're still standing afterward, still the same person you were before you looked. That's the whole exercise. It works because it breaks the pattern at the only point where the pattern is actually vulnerable — the moment of looking — and it proves, in your own body, that the verdict you were braced for doesn't arrive. The number arrives. You survive it. That's the data your nervous system actually needed, and no amount of thinking about it substitutes for having done it once.

One last thought before moving on: notice that none of the three overrides above asked you to become a fundamentally different person. They asked you to name a reflex, separate two ideas that had gotten stuck together, and look at one number. That's deliberately modest. The temptation, once you understand a pattern like this intellectually, is to try to overhaul everything at once — a new budgeting system, a complete personality shift around money, discipline summoned from nowhere by sheer force of insight. That approach rarely survives contact with a real Tuesday. What survives is small, repeatable, boring practice, done enough times that the nervous system actually updates instead of just the intellect. You don't need to become someone who loves looking at numbers. You just need to become someone who looks anyway.

The number was never what you were avoiding. You were avoiding who you'd have to be if you saw it — so see it anyway, and find out you're still you.

Chapter 3 — The Verdict You Already Reached

Why Checking Your Balance Feels Like a Trial, Not a Fact

It's ten-forty at night, the house quiet, everyone else already asleep, which is exactly when this particular ritual tends to happen — not in the busy, distracted middle of the day, but in the specific stillness right before sleep, when there's nothing left to hide behind and the mind, with nowhere else to go, finally turns toward the thing it's been circling all day. You told yourself you'd check "before bed," said it out loud even, to no one, the way you make small private promises you don't fully expect to keep.

You sit with the banking app open on your phone for eleven minutes without tapping the icon.

The screen has already gone dark twice. You wake it back up, thumb hovering, and in that hover you're not thinking about a number — you're thinking about what the number will say about you. Not "will there be enough to cover the card payment." You're further along than that already, deep into a trial that hasn't started collecting evidence yet. You're narrating a verdict: *if it's low, it means you're the kind of person who can't manage this. If it's really low, it means something worse — that you're careless, or behind, or fooling everyone who thinks you have it together.* You've built the entire courtroom before the first fact has entered as evidence.

You've been putting this specific check off for four days now, which doesn't sound like much until you notice how unlike you that is — you're someone who answers emails within the hour, who pays every other bill the day it arrives, who has a reputation among friends for being almost annoyingly on top of things. Four days of avoiding one single app doesn't fit that reputation, and some part of you has noticed the mismatch without being willing to look at it directly, the way you notice a strange sound in your car and immediately turn the radio up rather than investigate.

There's a small, almost comic detail worth including here, because it captures how absurd this all is once you can see it from outside: you have, at this exact moment, more than enough general financial literacy to explain overdraft protection to a friend, to calculate a tip, to compare interest rates on two competing offers. None of that competence is currently available to you. It's still there, technically, filed away correctly, but it's been temporarily locked out by a completely different system — the threat-detection system, which doesn't consult the financial-literacy system before it takes over, because as far as it's concerned, this isn't a financial situation. It's a verdict situation, and verdict situations get handled by fear, not arithmetic.

Notice what your body is doing while your thumb hovers. Shoulders up near your ears. Breath shallow, high in the chest, the kind of breathing that happens before a hard conversation, not before checking a number. Your jaw is tight enough that you'll feel it later, a dull ache you won't connect back to this moment. None of this is proportionate to what's actually about to happen — you're going to look at four or five digits on a screen — but proportion isn't the operating logic here. Threat is. And your body has already decided, eleven minutes before your thumb makes contact with the glass, that whatever's behind that icon qualifies.

You could, if pressed, tell yourself a perfectly reasonable story about why you haven't checked yet — you were tired, it's been a long week, there's no real urgency, tomorrow works just as well. Every piece of that story is individually true. None of it explains the specific, physical tightness in your chest, which doesn't respond to reasonable stories, because it was never generated by reasoning in the first place.

Eleven minutes is a long time to stand outside a door you could open with one thumb. But you're not stalling because you're lazy or forgetful. You're stalling because some part of you has already decided that what's behind that door isn't information. It's a verdict on who you are. And you'd rather live one more minute not-guilty than tap the icon and find out.

A third version of the same eleven minutes plays out for a man in his early thirties who isn't avoiding a balance at all, but a decision he's been putting off making — whether to accept a lower-paying job that would let him finally leave a workplace that's been eroding him for two years. He's run the budget seventeen times in his head and never once written it down, because writing it down would mean either confirming that the pay cut is survivable, in which case he'd have to actually face the harder, scarier work of quitting, or confirming that it isn't, in which case he'd have to sit with staying somewhere that's actively hurting him for reasons that are purely financial and therefore, in his mind, purely his own failure to have saved more, earned more, planned better. Either finished answer requires something of him he isn't ready to do. The unfinished, seventeen-times-recalculated version lets him keep feeling like he's working on it without ever having to act on what the math actually says. This is the eleven minutes stretched out over months instead of compressed into one evening — the same refusal to let a calculation finish, just given enough time to become a whole chapter of someone's life instead of one stalled Tuesday night.

A grandmother, sixty-eight, retired two years now, sits at her kitchen table with a Social Security statement and a pension letter spread in front of her, and she is doing the same eleven-minute stall in a different costume. She isn't avoiding an app. She's avoiding a specific piece of arithmetic: whether the number in front of her, combined with what's left of the savings she and her late husband built together, will actually last as long as she might. She has done this math before, roughly, in her head, on nights she couldn't sleep, and gotten an answer that frightened her enough that she's stopped doing it precisely on paper, because a rough, unfinished fear is somehow more bearable than a finished one. She tells her daughter she's "still figuring out the paperwork," which has been true, in the sense that the paperwork is still on the table, for four months. What she's actually protecting isn't a number. It's the version of herself that spent thirty years being the responsible one in her marriage, the one who managed the accounts, the one her husband trusted completely — and if the finished math says she miscalculated, that verdict doesn't just land on a spreadsheet. It lands on thirty years of a story about who she was to the person she loved most.

What's actually happening

The researcher Brené Brown has spent decades studying the difference between shame and guilt, and the distinction is the whole hinge of this chapter. Guilt says: *I did something bad.* Shame says: *I am bad.* Guilt is about behavior — a discrete, correctable, single event. Shame is about identity — global, total, and, crucially, not about any one thing you did. It's about who you supposedly *are* underneath everything you did.

That distinction sounds academic until you apply it to a banking app. If checking your balance triggered guilt, the process would be almost boring: you'd see the number, register "I overspent on X," and make a note to adjust. Guilt is specific. It points at an action and lets you fix the action. It has an exit.

Brown's research also identified something worth naming directly, because it explains why the eleven minutes feel so isolating even though almost everyone has lived some version of them: shame thrives specifically on secrecy, silence, and judgment, and it loses power fast in the presence of empathy — someone else saying, in effect, "me too." That's part of why this exact scene, the phone in hand, the screen going dark twice, rarely gets described out loud between friends, even close ones. People will tell you about a bad breakup, a health scare, a professional failure, almost performatively at this point — but the eleven minutes outside the banking app stay private, because shame convinces each person experiencing it that they're the only one, that everyone else checks their balance with the same unbothered ease they check the weather. They don't. Nearly everyone has stood in some version of this hallway. The particular cruelty of shame is how effectively it hides that fact from each person standing in it.

Shame doesn't have an exit, because shame was never really about the number. Shame takes one data point — a checking account balance, a credit card statement, a "you have $340 until payday" — and metabolizes it into a referendum on your entire character. Not "I overspent this month." Instead: "I am the kind of person who can't be trusted with money." Not "this bill came at a bad time." Instead: "I am always behind, I am always going to be behind, this is just what's true about me."

This global quality is precisely what makes shame so much harder to metabolize than guilt in practice, even when the actual facts are identical. Guilt is bounded in time — it points at an action that happened on a specific day and can, in principle, be closed. Shame is unbounded, because it's not describing an event, it's describing a permanent character trait that supposedly explains not just this month's overspending but last year's too, and next year's, stretching backward and forward indefinitely from a single data point. A single checking-account number gets asked to carry the entire weight of a life story, which is an absurd amount of evidentiary burden for four or five digits to bear — and yet that's functionally the job shame assigns it, every single time you open the app.

That's the mechanism behind the eleven minutes. You are not afraid of a number. Numbers are neutral — they don't have opinions about you. What you're actually afraid of is the internal verdict you've pre-loaded, the one where a single figure becomes proof of a permanent identity. And here's the trap inside the trap: because shame feels like a fact about who you *are* rather than a report on what you *did*, it doesn't respond to being handled the way guilt does. You can't "fix" shame by paying down a balance, because shame was never really accounting for the balance. It was accounting for your worth. So the app stays closed. Not checking becomes the only available relief — the only way to stay, for one more day, not-guilty of being who you're afraid you are.

This is the mechanism the whole book keeps circling back to: the numbers you refuse to look at were never really about the numbers. They were about who you'd have to admit you are if you looked. Chapter 3 is where that sentence gets its clearest anatomy. Shame is the machinery that turns "a number" into "a self."

There's a further wrinkle worth naming, because it explains why the grandmother's rough, sleepless-night math feels safer than the finished version on paper. The psychologists Daniel Kahneman and Amos Tversky, in their foundational work on judgment under uncertainty, documented that people often prefer a known, bounded uncertainty to a precise, fixed fact — even when the fact might turn out better than feared. A vague sense of "it might not be enough" can be lived inside, argued with, hoped against. A completed calculation collapses all of that into a single number that either clears the bar or doesn't, with no more room for hope to operate. This is part of why finishing the math feels riskier than merely worrying about it: worry, unfinished, still contains possibility. The final number takes the possibility away, for better or worse, and something in the mind resists trading a survivable uncertainty for an unsurvivable certainty — even when, as is true more often than feared, the certainty turns out to be the better news.

What it costs you

The financial cost is the boring half, but it's real, so start there. A balance you won't check is a balance you can't manage. Fees compound in the dark. A subscription you forgot about keeps drafting. An account drifting toward overdraft keeps drifting, because drifting requires no action and looking requires facing the verdict. Every day the app stays closed is a day the actual, correctable, guilt-shaped problem — spent a bit too much on this, missed that one payment — gets to grow undisturbed, quietly, into something bigger than it needed to be. Shame doesn't just fail to fix the problem. It actively protects the problem's ability to grow, because looking is the one thing shame won't let you do.

But the identity cost is the one that does the lasting damage, and it's sneakier because it doesn't look like a cost at all — it looks like caution. Every time you close the app instead of opening it, you're not just avoiding information. You're casting a vote for a specific story about yourself: *I am someone who can't handle this.* And votes accumulate. Avoidance isn't neutral; it's evidence-generating. The more times you flinch from the number, the more the flinch itself starts to feel like proof that the number really would be as bad as you feared — otherwise, why would you keep running from it? You end up in a loop where the avoidance and the shame manufacture each other. Shame causes the avoidance. The avoidance, over time, starts to feel like confirmation of the shame. Neither one needs the actual number to keep going.

There's a quieter cost still, underneath both of those: you stop being able to trust your own read on your life. Someone who checks their balance regularly, even when it's bad, builds a kind of muscle — *I can look at hard things and still function.* Someone who doesn't check loses access to that muscle entirely. You start to suspect, somewhere below conscious thought, that you're not someone who can face things. Not just financial things. Things in general. That suspicion doesn't stay contained to your bank account. It leaks into how you approach conflict, health, decisions of any weight — anywhere a hard fact might be waiting on the other side of a door you could open with one thumb.

Consider what actually gets rehearsed, physically, in those eleven minutes of stalling. Your nervous system isn't practicing patience or diligence. It's practicing the exact motor sequence of approach-and-retreat — reaching toward the discomfort, then pulling back before contact, over and over, refining the retreat rather than the approach. Every uncompleted attempt makes the next uncompleted attempt slightly easier to execute and slightly harder to interrupt, the same way any unfinished habit loop strengthens through repetition even when what's being repeated is the failure to finish rather than the completion.

There's a smaller, related habit worth naming here too — the specific way avoidance narrows not just what you check, but what you let yourself ask. Someone caught in this pattern stops asking a partner directly "how are we doing financially," stops asking a manager directly "am I being paid fairly for this role," stops asking themselves directly "is this actually sustainable." The questions don't disappear. They just get smaller, vaguer, safer — "are we okay?" instead of "what's our actual number?" — because a vague question can only receive a vague, reassuring answer, and a vague, reassuring answer is exactly what someone avoiding a verdict is unconsciously engineering the conversation to produce.

This is worth taking seriously as a general-purpose skill, not just a money habit, because the transfer effect runs in both directions. People who practice facing hard financial facts regularly often report that other kinds of avoidance — a difficult conversation, a medical appointment they've been postponing, an overdue performance review at work — get slightly easier to face too, not because the domains are related, but because the underlying skill being practiced is the same one: staying present with an uncomfortable fact long enough to discover it's survivable. The eleven minutes outside the banking app aren't just costing you information about your balance. They're a rehearsal, repeated weekly, for staying in the room with anything hard. Avoid the app long enough, and you're not just avoiding a number. You're keeping the rehearsal from ever happening.

The overrides

It's worth pausing here to notice something about the structure of the trial you're running before you've even opened the app: it only has one possible outcome that counts. If the number turns out fine, the trial doesn't register a "not guilty" verdict and move on — it just quietly cancels itself, as if it had never convened, and you rarely give yourself credit for the anxious eleven minutes you just survived for nothing. If the number turns out bad, the trial delivers its verdict in full, and you carry it for days. This is a rigged court. It only ever produces evidence against you, never in your favor, because a good outcome doesn't get cross-examined the way a bad one does — it just gets absorbed silently as "oh good, that's fine" and forgotten within the hour. Part of what the overrides below are trying to do is even out that asymmetry: to make you notice the good verdicts as deliberately as the bad ones, so the trial stops being structurally biased against you before it's even heard the facts.

Name the courtroom before you open the app. Before you check any number — balance, statement, total — say out loud or in your head: "This is one data point, not a verdict." It sounds almost too simple to matter, but the sentence does real work: it interrupts the automatic slide from guilt-language ("I overspent") into shame-language ("I am bad with money") before that slide has a chance to complete. You are giving your nervous system a label for what's about to happen, and labeled experiences are less able to hijack you than unlabeled ones.

Translate the verdict back into a sentence, every time. Whatever number you see, write one sentence that describes only the action, never the identity. Not "I'm a mess." Instead: "I spent more than planned on eating out this month." This is the guilt/shame swap made concrete — you are physically forcing the global judgment back down into a specific, correctable claim about behavior. Do this enough times and it stops being a trick you perform and starts being how your mind reaches for the number automatically.

If you find the sentence keeps drifting back toward identity language no matter how you phrase it — "I spent too much because I'm someone who can't control herself around food delivery apps," say — that's useful information, not a failure of the exercise. It tells you exactly where the fusion is strongest, which is usually a good map of where to focus the rest of this book's overrides first. The goal isn't a perfect, clean sentence on the first try. It's noticing, each time, exactly how far the identity language has crept in, and gently walking it back one more inch than the time before.

The Move: set a standing weekly check-in — same day, same five minutes, no exceptions, no reaction required. Pick a day. Sunday morning, Thursday lunch, whatever fits. The rule is: you open the app, you look at the number, and you close the app. No fixing required in that moment. No decisions required. The only job of the five minutes is looking. What this does is break the causal chain between *seeing* and *judging* — you're teaching your nervous system, on a schedule, that looking doesn't automatically trigger a verdict, because you've built a ritual where looking is followed by nothing except looking again next week. This is the text-a-friend version: "I check my balance every Sunday at 9am now, whether I want to or not, and it's stopped being scary." That's the line. That's the Monday-morning change — an actual five minutes on an actual calendar, not a mood you're hoping to eventually feel.

Finish the math you're doing halfway. If you notice yourself running a rough, worried version of a calculation in your head — again and again, always incomplete, never on paper — that's usually a sign the finished version is the thing you're actually protecting yourself from. Write it down fully, once, with real numbers, even if you have to guess at a few inputs. A completed calculation, even an imperfect one, almost always turns out to be more survivable than the open-ended dread it replaces, because dread has no floor and a number does.

One thing worth naming before moving to the next chapter: the weekly check-in above will feel, for the first several weeks, like something you're doing despite the fear rather than something that's dissolved the fear. That's normal, and it's not a sign the override isn't working. Fear doesn't respond to a schedule the first few times it's imposed on it — it responds to the accumulated evidence that the schedule produces over time. Give it six weeks before deciding whether this is helping. Most people report the eleven minutes shrinking to two or three by week four, and to something closer to a shrug by week eight.

The trial doesn't get dismissed by argument. It gets dismissed by a long enough run of verdicts that never arrive.

The number was never what you were avoiding. **A balance is a fact about last month; shame just wants you to read it as a verdict on who you are — check it anyway, translate it back into a sentence about behavior, and let the verdict starve.**

Chapter 4 — The Family Weather

Why the Money Story You Inherited Still Runs the Room

It's a Wednesday, nothing special about it, dinner not yet started, the specific low-key domestic hour where small logistical questions usually pass between you without any weight attached to them at all — who's picking up the dry cleaning, whether the dog's been fed, what time the appointment is tomorrow. This particular question landed in that same register, at least on your partner's end.

You flinch before you know why.

Your partner is standing in the kitchen with the laptop open, credit card statement on the screen, and their voice is completely level. "Hey, did you know what this charge from the pharmacy was?" That's it. That's the whole sentence. No edge in it. But something in your chest has already dropped six inches, and your hands have gone slightly cold, and for a half-second you are not in your kitchen at all. You are eight years old at a different table, and your mother is holding an envelope she hasn't opened yet, and the air in the room has gone thin and careful the way it always did on the third of the month. Nobody said anything was wrong. Nobody had to. You knew from the set of her jaw that this was not a conversation, it was a weather system, and weather systems were survived, not discussed.

You remember specific things about that table without ever having tried to memorize them — the way the overhead light hummed slightly, the particular blue of the envelope, the sound your mother's chair made when she finally stood up and put the envelope, still sealed, on top of the refrigerator, where it would sit for four more days. You remember that no one ate dessert that night, though nobody said why, and that when you asked, at nine years old, if everything was okay, you got a "we're fine, sweetheart" delivered in a voice that didn't match the word "fine" at all — a voice pulled thin and careful, holding something back you couldn't name and weren't supposed to ask about twice. You learned, in that kitchen, without a single direct lesson, that money trouble was a thing that happened in the room but was never allowed to be discussed in the room. The silence wasn't empty. It was the loudest part of the whole scene.

You come back to your own kitchen a second later. Your partner is still waiting for an answer about a $34 pharmacy charge. You've answered too fast, too clipped, with a note in your voice that doesn't belong to this moment at all. They blink. "I was just asking," they say, and now you have to explain a reaction that came from a different house, a different decade, a different woman entirely — except you can't, because you didn't know it was happening until it already had.

You apologize, awkwardly, and they say it's fine, and the conversation moves on to what the charge actually was — a prescription refill, nothing mysterious — and within two minutes everyone's back to normal, dinner gets made, the evening continues exactly as it would have if none of this happened. Except something did happen. Your body ran an old emergency protocol in response to a question that carried zero actual threat, and it did this so fast and so completely that by the time your conscious mind caught up, the reaction was already out in the room, already landed on your partner's face as a small flinch of confusion. This is the part that's hard to explain to someone who didn't grow up in a house with the same weather:

it wasn't a choice. There was no moment where you decided how to respond and picked wrong. The response arrived pre-loaded, the way a reflex arrives, faster than the thinking part of you could have vetoed it even if it had wanted to.

This is not about the $34. It was never about the $34. What just moved through your body is thirty years old, and it arrived before your thinking did.

A third household produces a third climate, and it's worth naming because it's the one that gets missed most often: the house where there wasn't much money and everyone talked about it constantly, but always with humor, always with a kind of defiant lightness that made scarcity into a running joke rather than a source of dread. A man in his thirties remembers his mother making a game out of counting change for the laundromat, remembers his family's "big spender" jokes on the rare nights they could afford takeout, remembers genuinely happy childhood memories built directly around not having much. He'd tell you, and mean it, that money wasn't a source of shame in his house at all — it was just a fact, handled with warmth. And yet, as an adult with a solid income, he still can't spend on himself without an automatic internal joke deflecting the expense before anyone else can — "living large tonight," he'll say, buying a sandwich, in the exact rhythm his mother used forty years ago about a bag of secondhand clothes. The joke isn't shame in the usual sense. But it's still a script, absorbed just as early, just as thoroughly, dictating that spending on himself requires a verbal apology dressed as humor before it's allowed to happen. Even the warmest inheritance still installs a script. It just installs a gentler one.

A different house produces a different weather, but the same climate. A woman in her late twenties grew up not in silence but in noise — her father talked about money constantly, openly, almost obsessively, narrating every purchase as a moral event. "That's a want, not a need." "You know what that costs in hours of my life?" Money was never hidden in her house. It was omnipresent, moralized, weaponized in small ways at every dinner, every birthday, every back-to-school shopping trip that came with a running commentary on sacrifice. She grew up financially literate in a technical sense — she can build a spreadsheet, she understands compound interest, she was taught more explicitly about money than most of her friends. And she also cannot buy herself something modest and enjoyable — a coffee, a dress, a plant for her apartment — without a small, automatic prosecutor's voice narrating the purchase back to her in her father's cadence, tallying its cost against some invisible ledger of worthiness. Her weather wasn't silence. It was surveillance. But it produced the identical result: money stopped being a neutral fact of daily life and became a stage where she was always, quietly, on trial.

What's actually happening

Children are not taught money. They are marinated in it. Long before anyone sits a kid down to explain what a bill is, that kid has already absorbed hundreds of hours of data about what money *feels like* in their house — whether it can be mentioned at dinner, whether it makes a parent's shoulders climb toward their ears, whether it is a subject that gets a door closed on it or a subject that gets discussed in the light. This is what psychologist Albert Bandura's work on social learning established decades ago: people acquire behavior largely by observing others, not by being instructed — and what gets modeled isn't just the action, it's the emotional charge that surrounds it. A child doesn't need to be told "money is dangerous." They just need to watch a parent's face change when the mail arrives.

Bandura's research also emphasized something particularly relevant here: modeling is most powerful when it comes from someone the observer identifies with closely, and when the same behavior is repeated consistently across many instances rather than shown once. A parent's careful, closed-off reaction to money wasn't a single data point you happened to notice once, at age eight. It was a pattern, reinforced dozens or hundreds of times across years, delivered by the two people in the world you were most primed to model yourself after. That's a very different kind of learning than a single bad memory. A single bad memory can be examined, contextualized, filed as unusual. A pattern repeated hundreds of times across your entire childhood doesn't get filed as a memory at all. It gets absorbed as the baseline — as simply how money is, the way gravity is simply how the world is, not a fact you were taught but a fact you've never known the world without.

There's a detail in this scene worth returning to, because it explains why the reaction was so total and so instantaneous: your body didn't just remember the feeling of that kitchen. It remembered the specific sensory package attached to it — the hum of the light, the color of the envelope, the exact texture of the silence — all of it stored together as a single unit, the way trauma researchers describe emotionally charged memories being encoded differently than ordinary ones, with sensory detail and emotional intensity fused so tightly that retrieving one retrieves the other automatically. Your partner's neutral tone was enough of a partial match to that stored package to trigger the whole thing at once, faster than conscious recognition, which is exactly why you were standing in your own kitchen and somewhere else entirely in the same half-second.

The financial-therapy researchers Brad Klontz and Ted Klontz (later joined by Sonya Britt) built on this idea with what they call money scripts — the largely unconscious beliefs about money that people absorb in childhood and then carry, unexamined, into their adult financial lives. Their research found that these scripts often form before age seven and predict financial behaviors decades later, independent of income or education. The scripts aren't facts. Nobody hands a seven-year-old a thesis statement about scarcity. What gets transmitted is tone, timing, and silence: the way a parent's voice went flat when a number came up, the way certain envelopes disappeared into a drawer instead of being opened at the table, the way asking "are we okay?" got a too-quick "we're fine" that made the asking feel like the actual offense.

That's the mechanism your body just ran in the kitchen. You weren't reacting to your partner. You were reacting to a *pattern-match* — their tone, the specific cadence of an unexpected money question, hit a template your nervous system built decades ago and never updated. The template says: money questions precede bad weather, bad weather must be minimized, minimizing looks like going quiet or going sharp, fast. You didn't choose that response. You inherited its wiring the way you inherited a jawline. And because it formed before you had language for it, it doesn't feel like a memory. It feels like an instinct. It feels like *just who you are around money* — which is exactly the trick. The family weather taught you a feeling and let you mistake it for a personality trait.

Sit with what the child version of you actually had access to in that moment — no context for what the envelope contained, no understanding of the actual financial stakes, nothing to work with except tone, posture, and the sudden absence of dessert. From that thin, sensory-only evidence, a whole operating theory got built: money trouble means silence, silence means safety, silence is the correct response to any financial threat. That theory was constructed by an eight-year-old with almost no real information, using the only tools an eight-year-old has — and it's been running, largely unexamined, in an adult's kitchen for decades since, still operating on the same thin evidence it started with.

This is worth distinguishing from a simpler, more familiar idea — that people just "repeat what they saw growing up." That framing makes it sound like a conscious imitation, a choice made in adulthood to model a parent's behavior. What's actually happening is closer to a reflex arc than a decision: the template was built before your prefrontal cortex, the part of your brain that does deliberate reasoning, was even fully online. You weren't old enough, when the template formed, to evaluate it, question it, or decide whether you wanted it. It got installed the way a first language gets installed — not chosen, not taught in the way arithmetic is taught, just absorbed through sheer repeated exposure during the exact developmental window when absorption is easiest and hardest to later override.

Here is the part worth sitting with: your parents almost certainly weren't trying to teach you anything. Most people who pass down a shame-and-silence pattern around money learned it exactly the same way — absorbed, not chosen, from a caregiver who was doing their best imitation of *their* caregiver. Nobody in that chain sat down and decided "I will make my child afraid of financial conversations." The pattern is self-propagating, not intentional. That's what makes it so persistent. Intentional harm gets noticed and resisted. Absorbed atmosphere just gets *become*.

The woman with the narrating father illustrates a variation on this framework worth naming on its own. Researchers in this field identify not just money *avoidance* scripts — the silence-and-secrecy pattern — but also money *vigilance* and money *status* scripts. In those, the inherited belief isn't "don't look" but "every dollar is a moral referendum" or "your worth is visible in what you spend." Her father didn't teach her to avoid the number. He taught her that the number was always watching her back. The behavior looks opposite — she checks everything, obsessively, where the kitchen-table child avoids everything — but the underlying fusion is identical: money and self-worth were welded together so early and so thoroughly that neither of them can experience a dollar as just a dollar. One learned to look away from the verdict. The other learned to never stop hearing it read aloud.

What it costs you

The money cost is the more countable one: people who inherited a secrecy-and-avoidance script are less likely to check statements, less likely to have direct conversations with partners about shared finances, and more likely to let small problems compound into large ones simply because looking is the thing that's been conditioned as dangerous. A missed subscription, a fee that keeps recurring, a balance quietly creeping — these don't survive regular contact. They survive avoidance. And avoidance is precisely the skill the family weather trained you in.

There's a specific version of this cost that shows up at the level of a partnership rather than an individual, and it's worth naming because it's often the first place the inherited script becomes visible enough to actually address. Two people entering a relationship rarely inherited identical money weather — one may have grown up in silence, the other in open, frequent discussion, and neither realizes, until they're merged into shared finances, that their instinctive comfort levels around money conversation are simply incompatible defaults, not personality flaws in either of them. The partner who wants to talk about the budget weekly isn't controlling. The partner who goes quiet at the mention of a joint statement isn't hiding something sinister. They're both running scripts installed by rooms neither of them chose, decades before they met, and the friction between the two scripts often gets misread as a character judgment about the relationship itself, when it's really just two different childhood climates trying to coexist in one adult kitchen.

But the quieter cost is the one that shows up in your kitchen and not on your bank statement. It's the tax on your closest relationship. Your partner asked a neutral question and got a defensive flinch they didn't cause and can't fix, because the real source of it is thirty years and one household away from them. Do that enough times — the snapped answer, the sudden chill, the subject-change that arrives a half-beat too fast — and your partner learns something too: that money is not a subject you two discuss like adults, it's a subject you two *manage around*, the same careful weather-watching you learned as a child, now running in a second household, teaching it to your own kids in turn if you have them. You didn't just inherit the pattern. Left alone, you're the delivery mechanism for handing it to the next kitchen table.

There's a specific, cumulative erosion that happens to trust in a long relationship when this pattern runs unexamined for years. It isn't dramatic — no single flinch ends anything. But a partner who's been on the receiving end of unexplained defensiveness around money for a decade eventually starts adjusting their own behavior around it, without necessarily naming what they're doing: bringing up financial topics less often, softening every question into something almost apologetic, quietly building their own parallel comfort with the household's numbers because direct conversation has come to feel like walking into weather. That adjustment looks, from the outside, like a healthy, low-conflict marriage. It's often something closer to a slow withdrawal from one specific room of shared life — a room that could have stayed open, if the flinch had ever gotten named instead of just managed around.

There's an identity cost underneath that too. Every time the old reaction fires and you don't catch it, you get a little more evidence for a story that isn't even true — *I'm just bad with money conversations, I'm just someone who gets weird about this.* That's not a fact about you. It's a thirty-year-old recording playing on a modern speaker. But if you never name it as a recording, you'll keep mistaking it for your voice.

And there's a cost that lands specifically on your children, if you have them, or will. Kids are the same kind of sensitive instrument you once were — marinating, not being taught. If your kitchen carries the same weather your childhood one did, even in a milder form, even with none of the original harshness, they will absorb the same lesson from the same source: that money is a subject the air in the room changes around. You don't have to repeat your parents' exact words for the pattern to transmit. The tone alone is enough. This is the part of the cost that compounds across generations rather than just years — not a debt you're carrying, but one you might still be handing forward without ever deciding to.

Here's the part worth sitting with longest: this pattern is genuinely reversible, and reversing it doesn't require a dramatic confrontation with your past or a single cathartic breakthrough. It requires something much smaller and more repeatable — noticing the flinch, one time, and choosing a different half-second response than the one the old recording is offering. Do that once and nothing changes structurally. Do it fifty times across a year, in fifty small kitchen moments nobody else will ever know were significant, and the recording genuinely does start to lose its grip, not because you argued it away but because you built enough new evidence, new responses, new proof that a money question can just be a money question, that the old track stops being the only track available. Your kids, if you have them, will absorb whichever version wins that quiet, ongoing contest. It's worth making sure it's the newer one.

The overrides

It's worth saying plainly, before the overrides, what this chapter is not arguing: it isn't arguing that your parents were villains, or that the weather in your childhood kitchen was unforgivable, or that understanding the pattern means you now owe anyone a confrontation. Most family money weather is generational fog, not malice — a pattern of fear and silence handed down by people who were themselves handed the same fog by their own parents, none of whom sat down and chose it. The goal here isn't blame. It's inventory. You're not trying to figure out who's at fault for the climate you grew up in. You're trying to figure out which parts of that climate you're still, unconsciously, carrying into rooms it was never built for — your own kitchen, your own partnership, your own kids if you have them — so you can decide, deliberately, which parts to keep and which to finally set down.

Name the room, not the number. The instant you feel that drop-in-the-chest reaction to a money question, say out loud — to yourself or to the person in front of you — "this isn't about the charge, this is old." One sentence. It doesn't need to be a confession or a therapy session in the kitchen. It just needs to interrupt the automatic handoff from *feeling* to *reaction* long enough for you to answer the actual question in front of you instead of the one from thirty years ago.

Ask your parent (or yourself) the plain question, once. If the relationship allows it, ask directly: "Growing up, could we talk about money at home, or did it feel like something to avoid?" You're not looking for an apology or an explanation. You're looking for confirmation that the weather pattern was real, because naming a thing you've only ever *felt* is what turns it from your personality into a documented family habit — one you can now consciously choose to keep or drop.

Be prepared for the conversation to surprise you in either direction. Sometimes a parent will confirm the pattern immediately and with real self-awareness — "yes, my parents never talked about it either, and I swore I'd be different and then somehow wasn't." Sometimes a parent will have no memory of the weather at all, genuinely unaware of the climate they created, which can itself be useful information: it confirms the pattern was absorbed rather than intended, transmitted below the level either of you consciously controlled. Either answer does the same job. It moves the pattern from an invisible, ambient fact of your personality into a named, historical event with an origin — and named things, unlike ambient ones, can actually be examined and revised.

The Move: schedule the exact conversation you're avoiding, for a neutral hour, before you need to. Not "we should talk about money sometime" — an actual fifteen minutes, on the calendar, this week, at a time when nobody's tired or already annoyed. Say to your partner: "Can we look at the card together Thursday at 7, just the two of us, nothing's wrong, I just want it to be normal for us to look." The content of that conversation matters less than the fact that you scheduled it *before* the tension arrived. A planned, low-stakes conversation about money, repeated a few times, is how a nervous system learns a new pattern: this doesn't have to be weather. It can just be a Thursday.

Separate the vigilance from the value. If your inheritance was narration rather than silence — a voice that tallied every purchase — practice buying one small, unremarkable thing without narrating it back to yourself in that old voice. Notice the prosecutor's commentary arrive, and instead of arguing with it, just note: "that's the old voice, not a fact about this purchase." You're not trying to silence thirty years of programming in one grocery run. You're just proving, once, that a fourteen-dollar candle doesn't require a verdict.

One more thing worth carrying forward: changing the climate in your own kitchen doesn't require your parents to change, apologize, or even understand what you're doing differently. This is a relief for people whose family of origin isn't available for repair — a parent who's passed away, or estranged, or simply not someone who'll ever be capable of the kind of conversation Chapter 4's second override describes. The work here doesn't run through them. It runs through you, in your own house, in real time, the next time a money question arrives and your body reaches for the old script. You can build a new climate without a single conversation with the people who built the old one. The weather you're responsible for now is the one in the room you're standing in.

You didn't choose the forecast you grew up under — but you get to decide whether your own kitchen keeps the same climate.

Chapter 5 — The Company You Keep Score With

Why Comparison Turns Your Numbers Into a Ranking

You leave your friend Marisol's dinner and the night was good — laughter, a decent bottle of wine someone brought, her husband's terrible pun about the pasta — and then somewhere between the front door and your car, without deciding to, you start doing math. She mentioned the kitchen. Not bragging, just mentioning it, the way you mention things that are simply true about your life now: the contractor, the backsplash, the six weeks of takeout while it happened. You nod along at the time. It's only later, alone with the seatbelt clicking into place, that the number arrives uninvited — what that probably cost, stacked against what's sitting in your account, and the stack doesn't favor you.

The strange part is how genuinely happy you were for her during the actual conversation. There was no performance in your congratulations, no gritted-teeth politeness — you meant it, you were glad, the kitchen really is beautiful and she really does deserve it after the year she's had. The comparison didn't arrive during the warmth. It arrived after, in the quiet, once the social performance of being a good friend had ended and there was nothing left to do but sit with your own thoughts in a parked car. That's often when the ledger opens — not in the room with the person, where connection is doing its job, but in the after-space, where connection has nothing left to compete with.

You've known Marisol for eleven years — met in a shared apartment building in your twenties, both broke in roughly the same way at the time, both eating the same cheap pasta on the same folding table more nights than either of you would now admit to. That history is doing something specific in the background of tonight's comparison: it gives the current gap between her kitchen and your own a felt sense of trajectory, a before-and-after, in a way a stranger's renovation never could. It's not just "she has something I don't." It's "we started in the same place, and now we don't," which is a much sharper, more personal cut than the first version, even though the underlying facts — a kitchen, a countertop, a contractor — are identical either way.

You don't know what she owes on the house. You don't know if the renovation was financed, gifted, timed against a bonus, or quietly draining a savings account she'll be anxious about for years. You know none of the load-bearing facts. You know the counters were quartz and yours are not, and somehow that single visible fact outvotes every invisible one. By the time you're home you feel, specifically, poor — not in a number sense, in a *self* sense, like something about who you are got smaller over the course of one dinner.

You lie in bed running the numbers you don't actually have — guessing at Marisol's household income, guessing at what the contractor probably charged, building an entire financial biography for a friend based on a granite countertop and a story about takeout. None of this math is real. You're not solving anything. You're constructing a scoreboard out of fog, and then reading your own position on it as if the scoreboard were solid ground. And the strange part, if you could step back and watch yourself do this from a slight distance, is how much effort goes into a calculation you'd never accept from anyone else. If a stranger told you they knew for certain how much money a family had, based only on the material of their kitchen counters, you'd immediately point out the obvious gaps in that reasoning. You'd never accept that as valid evidence in an argument. And yet here, at midnight, doing this math about someone you love, the same reasoning sails through completely unchallenged, because it isn't actually functioning as reasoning. It's functioning as a feeling wearing reasoning's clothes. Your partner asks what's wrong and you say "nothing, just tired," because "I'm doing imaginary math about our friend's kitchen" sounds, said out loud, exactly as absurd as it is — and yet in the dark, in your head, it didn't feel absurd at all. It felt like an urgent piece of information you needed to process before you could sleep.

This is not sadness about a kitchen. This is your mind doing something it does constantly and almost never announces: it grabbed the nearest person and used them as the ruler.

Notice the specific sequence of events, because the sequence is the tell. The sting didn't arrive during the mention of the kitchen itself — you were fine in that moment, genuinely engaged, asking a follow-up question about the contractor with real curiosity. It arrived later, alone, once the social task of being a good dinner guest had ended and your mind had nothing left to occupy it except its own comparisons. This is a pattern worth remembering: the comparison rarely does its damage in company. It waits for the quiet, and does its work there, uninterrupted, where no one else's presence can dilute it.

What makes this particular ruler so deceptive is how selectively it operates. You didn't run this same math on the friend at the same dinner who mentioned, offhand, that she's still renting a room from a college friend at thirty-six because buying feels permanently out of reach. You didn't run it on the friend whose small business had a rough year and who ordered the cheapest thing on the menu without comment. Your mind didn't grab either of them as the ruler, even though both were sitting at the exact same table, offering the exact same amount of comparison-relevant information. It grabbed Marisol, specifically, because Marisol's news happened to point in the direction the ruler is always secretly biased toward — upward, toward threat, toward the version of the evening that could make you feel behind. The ruler isn't neutral. It's rigged to find the one comparison in the room that stings, and ignore the two that would have soothed, and it does this so smoothly you never notice it made a selection at all.

A sixty-year-old man runs the same comparison engine at the opposite end of life, standing at a colleague's retirement party listening to a toast that mentions, in passing, the colleague's plans to spend six months a year at a place in another country. He does the math instantly and involuntarily — what that kind of retirement requires, set against his own accounts, which he has checked recently enough to know are solid but not that solid, not "six months abroad" solid. He smiles through the toast. He means the smile; he likes this colleague, is genuinely glad for him. But he drives home doing an entirely different kind of arithmetic than the twenty-four-year-old with the washer-dryer — not "am I keeping up," but something heavier: "did I make the wrong choices, thirty years ago, that are only now, at the finish line, going to show." Comparison doesn't get gentler with age or income. It just changes what it's measuring against, from a studio apartment to a decade of decisions that can no longer be revised.

A twenty-four-year-old grad student runs the identical program at a much smaller scale, standing in a friend's studio apartment noticing it has a washer-dryer in the unit — hers doesn't — and feeling something small and sour move through her that has no reasonable relationship to what a washer-dryer actually costs to add to a monthly rent. She knows, rationally, that her friend's parents likely cosigned the lease, that this is a difference measured in a few hundred dollars a month, that in five years it will mean nothing at all. None of that knowledge stops the feeling from arriving anyway, small and immediate, the moment her eyes land on the machine. It isn't really about laundry. It's the same mechanism running at student-budget scale: a visible detail became a stand-in for a comprehensive verdict on whose life is more together, and the comparison landed before she'd consented to make it.

What's actually happening

The psychologist Leon Festinger proposed something in the 1950s called social comparison theory, and the core idea is almost embarrassingly simple once you see it: humans don't have a built-in, absolute gauge for how well they're doing.

There's no internal dial that reads "fine" against some fixed universal standard. Instead, you figure out how you're doing by looking sideways — at the people around you — and measuring the gap.

This isn't a flaw bolted onto an otherwise rational system. It's the system. Festinger's insight was that comparison is often the *only* tool available for self-evaluation, especially for things that don't come with an objective scoreboard. "Am I doing okay financially" doesn't have a universal answer key the way "how tall am I" does. So the mind reaches for the nearest available comparison and treats it as the answer key instead.

Festinger also noted something that's easy to overlook: people don't compare themselves against just anyone. They compare themselves preferentially against people who are similar to them along dimensions that matter — same rough age, same profession, same social tier, same starting point in life. This is precisely why a stranger's mansion glimpsed on television produces almost no sting at all, while a close friend's kitchen renovation produces a real one. The mansion is too far outside your reference group to register as a meaningful comparison; some part of you correctly files it as belonging to a different category of life entirely, celebrity or inherited wealth or simply not-the-same-game. Marisol is exactly close enough — same rough starting point, same era of life, someone you've watched build a career alongside your own — that the comparison lands as relevant, as *applicable to you specifically*, in a way a stranger's yacht never could. The closer the peer, the sharper the sting. That's not a coincidence. That's the mechanism working exactly as it evolved to.

Consider how strange it would sound if this same mechanism ran on something with an actual objective answer key — imagine feeling worse about your own height because a friend happened to be taller, or feeling like a worse parent because a friend's toddler slept through the night first. In domains with clear, external measures, comparison mostly just informs; it doesn't devastate, because there's a stable ground truth underneath it that comparison can't distort. Money has no such ground truth in most people's felt experience, no clean external answer key that says definitively "you're fine" or "you're not." That absence is exactly what leaves the door open for a stranger's kitchen counter to walk in and answer a question it was never equipped to answer.

Two things make this especially dangerous with money specifically. First, financial life is almost entirely invisible. You cannot see someone's debt, their parents' help, their divorce settlement, their 90-hour weeks, their fear. You can only see the kitchen. Which means every comparison you make is a comparison between your *whole, known, messy truth* and someone else's *edited, visible surface*. That is not a fair fight. It was never going to be.

Second, the direction of the comparison matters enormously, and your mind defaults to the worse one. Researchers who've built on Festinger's original framework distinguish between "downward" comparisons — measuring yourself against someone doing worse, which tends to soothe — and "upward" comparisons — measuring yourself against someone who appears to be doing better, which tends to sting. Left unmanaged, attention drifts upward. You don't leave dinner thinking about the friend who's still renting a room at thirty-nine. You think about the one with the kitchen. The mind is drawn to the comparison that produces the most information about threat, and a threat to your standing registers as more urgent than a comfort about it — so it's the upward comparisons that get replayed on the drive home, not the downward ones.

There's an evolutionary logic underneath this asymmetry that's worth naming, because it explains why the upward pull feels so involuntary. In an environment where social standing determined access to resources, allies, and mates, accurately tracking who was rising relative to you wasn't vanity — it was survival-relevant information, worth paying close, anxious attention to. The machinery that runs the checkout-line comparison and the dinner-party comparison alike is very old machinery, built for a world of small, visible tribes where everyone's relative position was common knowledge and mattered enormously. That machinery hasn't updated for a world of social media feeds and casually mentioned kitchen renovations, where you're now exposed to thousands of potential upward comparisons a week instead of the handful a small tribe would have generated in a lifetime. The mechanism isn't broken. It's just wildly, catastrophically over-fed.

Put those two things together — invisible inputs, upward-skewed attention — and you get a machine custom-built to manufacture a deficit that may not even exist. You don't know if you're behind Marisol. You only know you *feel* behind, and the feeling arrived so fast and felt so much like fact that you never thought to ask it for its sources.

This is the thread running under everything in this book: the numbers you avoid were never really about the numbers. They were about who you'd have to admit you are if you looked. And comparison is one of the sneakiest ways that avoidance disguises itself as information — you tell yourself you're "seeing where you stand," when actually you're just importing someone else's highlight reel and calling it a scoreboard.

There's a further piece of this worth naming, because it explains why the sting fades so slowly. The psychologist Robert Zajonc's research on the "mere exposure effect" found that repeated exposure to something, on its own, increases how favorably we regard it — familiarity breeds a kind of automatic warmth. The dark twin of that effect shows up in comparison: repeated exposure to a peer group's visible wealth doesn't just produce one sting per dinner, it recalibrates your entire sense of "normal." If everyone in your regular circle drives a newer car, the newer car quietly becomes the baseline your mind measures against, even though the actual baseline — what a comfortable, reasonable life costs — hasn't moved an inch. Your reference point drifted because your circle's visible surface did, and the drift is invisible from inside it. You don't notice your baseline moving. You just notice, one day, that a car that would have felt like plenty five years ago now quietly feels like falling behind.

What it costs you

The money cost is the more forgivable one, and it's real: comparison-driven spending is a documented, common pattern — the sense of falling behind a visible peer often prompts a purchase that has nothing to do with need and everything to do with closing the gap you just imagined. A renovation you weren't planning. A dinner out you can't quite afford, booked the week after the one where you felt small. None of these purchases are aimed at anything you actually wanted before the comparison happened. They're aimed at the feeling, and feelings are expensive to chase because they never stay caught.

What makes comparison-driven spending especially costly, compared to other kinds of impulse spending, is that it's aimed at closing a gap that was never accurately measured in the first place. You're not spending to acquire something you specifically want. You're spending to erase a feeling of relative deficit built on incomplete information — and because the deficit was fictional to begin with, no purchase can actually close it. You can match the kitchen, or the car, or the vacation, and the relief will last exactly as long as it takes for the next visible marker to appear in someone else's life, because the underlying mechanism — measuring your worth against a moving, partially invisible target — was never actually addressed by the purchase. This is why comparison spending has a specific, recognizable shape over time: not one large purchase that resolves things, but a long, low drip of smaller ones, each chasing a target that relocates the moment it's reached.

But the quieter cost is worse, and it's this: comparison teaches you to locate your worth in a ranking rather than a life. Every dinner becomes a data point. Every casual mention of a vacation, a raise, a new car in someone's driveway becomes something to silently process and file under "ahead" or "behind." You stop being able to just enjoy your friend's good news, because some part of you is running a background calculation about what it means for you. That's a specific kind of loneliness — being surrounded by people you love while quietly scoring yourself against them. You showed up for the pasta and the pun and Marisol's actual company, and you left having mostly had dinner with a spreadsheet.

And because the comparison is built on partial information, the ranking it produces is fiction dressed as fact. You are grieving a status you don't actually hold, based on math you don't have the numbers to do. That's a strange kind of cost — paying an emotional price for a debt you were never actually issued.

There's also a corrosive effect on the friendship itself that's easy to miss because it happens entirely on your side of the relationship. Marisol didn't do anything to you. She mentioned a kitchen renovation the way you'd mention any true fact of your life to a friend you trust. If the comparison you ran in the car starts showing up as subtle distance the next time you see her — a slight reluctance to ask follow-up questions about the renovation, a flicker of relief when she mentions a setback, a preference for spending time with friends whose lives look less finished than yours — that's the ranking doing real damage to a relationship that never asked to be a scoreboard. The friendship pays a price for a comparison the friendship never consented to.

There's a final cost worth naming, one that operates on a longer horizon than any single evening: repeated upward comparison, left unexamined, tends to narrow a life rather than expand it. People who feel chronically behind a peer group don't typically respond by taking bigger, bolder financial risks to catch up — they usually respond by shrinking, spending less on genuine enjoyment, socializing less with the very friends whose success stings, quietly opting out of experiences that might surface another uncomfortable data point. The comparison that was supposed to be information about where you stand ends up functioning as a fence, and the fence gets built entirely by you, around a life that was never actually threatened by anything except a feeling you never fact-checked.

The overrides

There's a broader pattern worth naming before the overrides, because it will save you from a trap the overrides alone won't catch: comparison doesn't only run on wealth. It runs on anything visible and rankable — career trajectory, who got married first, whose kids are hitting which milestones, who looks like they're aging better, who seems calmer, more settled, more finished as a person. Money is just the most countable version of a much larger habit, which means fixing your relationship to Marisol's kitchen won't fully solve the deeper pattern if the same ranking instinct is still running unchecked in every other domain of your life. The overrides below are written for money specifically, because that's this book's subject, but notice, as you practice them, whether the same reflex is showing up elsewhere too — at a school reunion, in a sibling's success, in a friend's relationship that looks, from the outside, easier than yours. The mechanism doesn't care what it's ranking. It just wants a ruler.

Name the comparison out loud, the moment you notice it. Not analyze it — just name it. "I'm comparing myself to

Marisol's kitchen right now." Said out loud or even just formed clearly as a sentence in your head, this does something small but real: it moves the comparison from *felt fact* to *observed thought*. Festinger's whole framework depends on the comparison happening automatically, beneath notice. The instant you notice it, it loses its authority. It becomes a thing your mind is doing, not a verdict about your life.

The Move: before you let a comparison finish landing, ask it one question — "What do I actually not know here?" Then list it. You don't know what she owes. You don't know if it's financed. You don't know what she's afraid of at 2 a.m. You don't know her parents didn't help. Do this three or four times and you'll notice the list is always long and the visible fact — the kitchen — is always short. This isn't about deciding she's secretly worse off; it's not a game of "actually I probably win." It's about correctly sizing how little the visible surface tells you, so the comparison stops being able to pose as complete information.

Keep a running version of this list somewhere you'll actually see it again — a note on your phone, a line in a journal —

because the exercise gets more powerful with repetition and pattern-recognition. After doing it a dozen times across a dozen different comparisons, most people start to notice the same handful of unknowns recurring: financing, family help, hidden stress, timing against a bonus or windfall. Once you've seen the pattern enough times, the next comparison starts to trigger the corrective almost automatically, before the sting has time to fully land. That's the goal — not eliminating comparison, which isn't realistic, but shortening the window where it gets to operate as if it were complete information.

Build a standing appointment with your own numbers, not your neighbor's. Once a week, five minutes, same day, look at what's actually true for you — what you have, what you owe, what moved. This is the same move from setting up a low-stakes recurring money conversation instead of an ambush: a ranking built on someone else's visible edges only feels urgent because you haven't built a stronger, quieter habit of checking your own. When your own numbers are a known, familiar Thursday thing rather than a mystery, a stranger's kitchen has a lot less power to define you for an evening.

A closing thought worth holding onto: the goal here was never to stop noticing other people's lives — that would mean not caring about the people around you, which isn't the point and isn't healthy either. The goal is to stop letting the noticing automatically convert into a ranking. You can register that Marisol renovated her kitchen, feel genuinely happy for her, and simply not run the arithmetic that turns her good news into your bad news. That's not suppression. It's accuracy — refusing to let an incomplete data set masquerade as a verdict on your own life, while still staying fully, warmly present for the people you love.

Comparison will always find you a ranking. It just won't tell you it made half the numbers up.

Chapter 6 — The Mask That Costs More Than the Debt

Why Looking Fine Becomes More Urgent Than Being Fine

It's a Friday night, the kind this particular group has been doing monthly for almost three years now, the same six people, rotating restaurants, a standing tradition nobody formally organizes anymore because it just happens. Tonight it happened to be a slightly nicer place than usual — someone's idea, agreed to by group consensus, nobody objecting even though at least two people at the table, if being honest, felt a small private wince at the prices on the menu before ordering anyway.

Jon picks up the check before he decides to. His hand is already reaching for it while his mouth is still forming the sentence "let me get this one" — and somewhere behind his eyes, a second, quieter self is doing math it doesn't like. Four hundred and ten dollars. Split six ways would have been sixty-eight each, painless, forgettable. But somebody joked "just put it on Jon's card, he's the responsible one," and the table laughed, and the moment for correction closed like a door he didn't see swing shut. Now the card is out. Now the waiter is walking away with it. Now he is smiling and saying something about how it's no big deal, truly, please, while a number that will not fit anywhere in his account settles into his chest like a stone dropped into still water.

The joke wasn't even unkind. Everyone at that table would say, if asked, that they were teasing him with real affection — "he's the responsible one" is a compliment, the kind of label you earn by consistently being the guy who remembers reservations and tips well and never makes a scene about the bill. That's exactly the trap. The label was built, deposit by deposit, out of a hundred earlier moments where he did something similar and let it pass without correction, and now the label has a kind of gravity of its own — it pulls him toward behavior that confirms it, whether or not he can currently afford to confirm it. He built the reputation. Now the reputation is spending his money for him.

Somewhere around the third glass of wine, before the check even arrived, he'd already half-known this was coming — could feel the shape of the evening tilting toward the moment where someone would make the joke, where the group's easy assumption about who "handles" things would activate on cue, the way it always does. He could have preempted it. There was a window, maybe ninety seconds long, sometime between the entrées and the dessert menu, where a casual "let's just split evenly tonight" would have landed easily, unremarkably, forgotten by dessert. The window closed. It always closes faster than you expect.

He will feel the ripples of that stone for nine days. Not because anyone at the table will ever mention it again — they've already forgotten, already moved on to splitting a rideshare — but because he has to live inside the gap between what he just performed and what he can actually afford, and that gap doesn't close when the dinner ends. It just goes quiet. It waits in a notifications tab. It becomes the reason he says he's "not really feeling takeout this week," which is true, technically, in the way a symptom is technically a fact about a cause nobody's named.

What's strange is that nobody made him do this. No one held a number over his head. He held it over his own.

Watch the physical mechanics of it once more, slowed down: the hand moving before the sentence finishes, the reach outpacing the thought. That sequencing is the whole diagnosis in miniature. A deliberate, considered generosity would let the thought arrive first and the hand follow it. Here the order is reversed, which is exactly what happens when a behavior has been so thoroughly rehearsed it no longer requires conscious authorization — the body already knows its line before the mind has finished deciding whether it agrees with it.

It's worth naming exactly how invisible this is to everyone at the table, because that invisibility is doing real work. Nobody at dinner witnessed a struggle. From their side of the table, they watched a friend do something generous, easily, with a smile, the way he always does. The performance wasn't just successful — it was so successful it left zero evidence of having been a performance at all. This is different from most kinds of struggle, which at least sometimes show on a person's face, in a raised voice, in a visible tell. Financial performance can be, and often is, completely undetectable from the outside, which means the people who love you most can be sitting three feet away from a genuine moment of distress and never once suspect it happened. The mask isn't just hiding the number from a stranger. It's hiding it from the people best positioned to actually help.

A nineteen-year-old runs a smaller-stakes version of the identical mechanism, in a dorm room, deciding whether to join four roommates driving three hours for a concert — gas split, tickets, a hotel room split five ways that still comes to more than he has free that month. He says yes before he's done the math, the way you say yes reflexively to things your friend group has already decided are happening, because being the one who has to ask "how much, exactly?" marks you, instantly, as different — the poor friend, the one whose family situation is different, the one who has to think about money in a way the others visibly don't have to. He'll spend the drive there doing math he should have done before agreeing, and he'll come back having enjoyed the concert genuinely, and also having created a small, private financial hole he'll spend the next six weeks quietly filling, alone, telling no one, because at nineteen the fear of being marked as different from your friend group can feel more urgent than any number on a bank app.

A woman in her mid-thirties runs the same performance in a completely different register: the group chat for a friend's bachelorette weekend, three cities and a shared villa, and she types "I'm in!!" with genuine enthusiasm before she's looked at a single price, because the alternative — being the one who has to ask "how much, roughly?" before committing — feels like announcing something she isn't ready to announce to eleven women she's known since college. She spends the next six weeks in a low hum of financial anxiety that never once surfaces in the group chat, where she remains upbeat, engaged, first to react with an emoji to every logistics update. By the time the weekend arrives, she's put the flights on a card she's still paying off from last year, and she will, at some point during the trip, laugh generously at a joke about splitting the villa cost "evenly, obviously," while doing silent math that makes her stomach drop. The front held for six weeks. It always does, until the bill for maintaining it comes due somewhere else.

What's actually happening

The sociologist Erving Goffman spent much of his career describing something so ordinary that most people never notice they're doing it: every time you're in front of other people, you're performing a version of yourself, adjusting your face, your posture, your words, to fit the impression you're trying to create. He called this impression management, and the frame he built around it — dramaturgy — treats everyday life as a kind of stage. There's a front region, where you perform for an audience, and a back region, where you drop the performance and let your face rest. The dinner table is a front region. So is the group chat where you say "yeah I'm in" for the weekend trip before checking your balance. So is the parking lot of the gym where you hope no one notices your car is the oldest one there.

Here is the part Goffman was careful about that most people skip: performing a front isn't free. It takes ongoing effort to sustain — what he'd call "expressive control." You have to keep managing the details, keep the story consistent, keep the audience from seeing behind the set. In financial life, that ongoing effort has a literal price tag. Grabbing the check is spending to signal a front — I'm the one who can afford this, I'm not the kind of person who counts. Saying yes to the trip before you've checked anything is sustaining a front you built months ago and can't now retire without someone noticing the set change. Every one of these acts is a performance cost, and performance costs compound, because the front doesn't get easier to maintain over time — it gets more expensive, since each new performance has to top the last one or the illusion cracks.

Goffman also wrote about what he called "team performances" — situations where multiple people collaborate, often without discussing it, to sustain a shared impression. A group of friends who all consistently pick up rounds, split evenly regardless of who ordered what, upgrade vacations together year over year, are frequently performing a team front none of them individually chose and none of them would admit to feeling pressured by. Everyone privately assumes everyone else can afford it, because everyone else looks like they can, and nobody wants to be the first to break character and ask the group to scale down. The whole group can be, simultaneously, quietly stretched thin, each member convinced they're the only one struggling to keep pace with a standard the group invented by mutual, unspoken agreement — a standard that would evaporate instantly if even one person said the quiet part out loud.

This isn't vanity, and it isn't even really about money. Goffman's whole point was that the self you present in front of others feels, to you, like it might be revealed as false at any moment — and the fear of that exposure is what drives the performance harder, not the desire to impress. You don't grab the check because you want the table to admire you. You grab it because if you didn't, for one second, you'd have to sit inside the true fact of your numbers in front of witnesses, and that fact currently has no story you're ready to tell. Paying for the meal you can't afford is cheaper, in the moment, than being seen.

Goffman called this the fear of "losing face" — a term he took seriously as a technical concept, not just a figure of speech. Losing face, in his framework, isn't simply embarrassment. It's the specific, acute discomfort of having the version of yourself you've been presenting suddenly contradicted, in real time, in front of the very people who'd been accepting that presentation as true. What makes it so potent is the social nature of the exposure: it isn't just that you'd know the truth about your finances, which you already know privately and manage fine.

It's that everyone else would know it too, simultaneously, and you'd have to watch them re-file you in real time. That specific, socially-witnessed re-filing is what the check-grab is built to prevent, and it's a far more primal fear than simple financial anxiety — closer to the fear of social exile than the fear of a bad number.

The book's throughline sits exactly here. The numbers you refuse to look at were never really about the numbers — they were about who you'd have to admit you are if you looked. The dinner check isn't a check. It's a stand-in for the identity conversation you're avoiding, paid for in real currency because the emotional currency wasn't available.

The economists Richard Zeckhauser and William Samuelson identified a related pattern worth naming here — what they called the status quo bias, people's tendency to stick with a current arrangement even when a change would clearly serve them better, simply because change requires an active, visible decision while staying the same requires nothing but silence. Saying "yes I'm in" before checking a number is a status quo choice disguised as a decision: it keeps the current social arrangement — the one where you're seen as easy, game, unbothered by cost — undisturbed, while actually raising your objection later would require an active, visible break from that arrangement in front of witnesses. The bias isn't laziness. It's a real asymmetry in how costly the two options feel: staying silent costs you privately, later, alone; speaking up costs you publicly, now, in front of people whose opinion you're actively managing. Most people, most of the time, will choose the private cost. It's the one that doesn't have an audience.

What it costs you

Start with the money, because it's the easier half and it's not small. A person who covers the group dinner "just this once" a few times a year, buys the round of drinks to keep pace with a friend group's spending rhythm, upgrades to match a colleague's new car before their own has any real problem — that person can lose real, countable thousands a year to performance spending that produced zero enjoyment, because the entire point of performance spending is that you don't get to enjoy it. You can't relax into a purchase that exists to prevent a feeling. The steak at the dinner you couldn't afford doesn't taste like a treat. It tastes like a deadline.

But the identity cost is the one that does the lasting damage, and it's this: every successful performance teaches you that the performance works. You picked up the check, nobody noticed the flinch, the dinner ended, the world didn't end — so the front holds. And because it held, you now believe a little more strongly that the front is what's actually keeping you safe, rather than a costume draped over a problem that's still breathing underneath. The performance doesn't just cost money. It reinforces the exact avoidance that got you into needing a performance in the first place. Each time the mask works, looking underneath it gets a little more unthinkable — because now you'd have to explain not just the numbers, but why you spent a decade convincing everyone, including yourself, that there was nothing to explain.

There's a specific compounding cost to the fact that performance is *rewarded socially* in a way that honesty about limits usually isn't, at least not immediately. The dinner table laughed warmly at "he's the responsible one." Nobody claps for the version of that scene where he says "actually, can we split this evenly, I need to be careful this month." The visible incentives all point toward maintaining the front — praise, ease, a reputation people genuinely admire — while the cost of maintaining it stays invisible, deferred, felt only later and alone. This is a specific kind of trap: the social reward structure and the actual financial structure are pointing in opposite directions, and social rewards are immediate while financial consequences are delayed, which means the front will almost always win the moment-to-moment competition even in a person who fully understands, intellectually, that it's the wrong long-term trade. Knowing this doesn't automatically fix it. But it does explain why willpower alone rarely does either — you're not fighting a character flaw, you're fighting a reward schedule that's stacked against the honest choice every single time it comes up.

That's the quieter cost: the self behind the front gets less real to you, not more. Goffman's "back region" — the place where you drop the act and just are what you are — starts to shrink from disuse. If you've spent years managing the impression, you may genuinely struggle to answer, alone, with no one watching, what you actually want your financial life to look like. The performance was so demanding it crowded out the planning. You got very good at looking like someone with it handled. You never got around to handling it.

There's also a specific loneliness in successful performance that people rarely name, because it sounds like a strange thing to be sad about. If the front works — if nobody at the table ever suspects the check was a stretch — then nobody ever gets the chance to actually know you, the version with real constraints and real numbers, because that version was never presented. You can be surrounded by people who like you enormously and still be, in the one way that matters most, unknown to all of them. The performance that was meant to keep you safe from judgment also quietly keeps you from being met. That's a trade most people don't remember agreeing to.

There's also a version of this cost that lands specifically on the next financial decision you'll face, whatever it happens to be. A person who has spent years managing an expensive front rarely has an accurate baseline for what their actual, honest cost of living looks like, because so much of what they spend has been shaped by performance rather than preference. Ask him, honestly, what a comfortable month actually costs him if nobody were watching, and he may genuinely not know, because the number has been inflated by years of checks he didn't need to pick up and trips he didn't need to say yes to before checking anything. The mask doesn't just cost the specific dinner. It corrupts the underlying data he'd need to make good decisions about anything else — a budget, a big purchase, a career change that would mean a temporary pay cut — because the baseline itself was never honest to begin with.

The overrides

Before the overrides, it's worth being honest about something the chapter hasn't said outright yet: dropping the front is genuinely scary, and the fear isn't irrational. There is real social risk in being seen accurately. Some friendships really are conditional on a version of you that can keep pace, and finding that out is painful. But it's worth distinguishing between two different fears that tend to get bundled together — the fear that people will think less of you for being honest about money, and the fear that some relationships were never really about you in the first place. The first fear is usually oversized; most people, most of the time, respect honesty about money more than they respect a performance they can half-sense is strained. The second fear is sometimes accurate, and if it is, that's genuinely useful information about the relationship, learned far more cheaply through one honest sentence than through years of quietly overspending to avoid finding out.

The Move: before the next group expense lands — the dinner, the trip, the gift pool — say the true number out loud to one person, in advance, before you're in front of an audience. Not at the table. Before it. Text a friend going to the same dinner: "heads up, I'm going to do my own tab tonight, not up for splitting evenly." This works because it moves the disclosure out of the front region and into a smaller, safer back-region conversation, where you can say the true thing without an audience watching your face manage it in real time. Once it's said once, it's said. You don't have to perform around it at the table, because the table already knows the shape of the truth.

Second, install a twenty-four-hour rule specifically for reach-for-the-check moments — the exact instant your hand starts moving faster than your judgment. Say, lightly, "let's actually split this one," and if the moment has already passed and the card's already out, that's fine, this override is for next time. The rule isn't about this dinner. It's about breaking the automaticity — the hand moving before the mind agrees — by inserting one beat of hesitation where a decision used to happen for you.

The first few times you try this, expect it to feel disproportionately hard — a strange amount of internal resistance for what is, mechanically, just letting a bill get split the ordinary way. That resistance is the reputation defending itself, the same "he's the responsible one" gravity pulling your hand back toward the old pattern. Push through it anyway, and notice what actually happens afterward: usually nothing. The table splits the bill, the conversation moves on, nobody remembers it in a week. The catastrophe the reputation was warning you about essentially never arrives. That's worth banking as evidence for the next time the old pull shows up.

Third, once a month, deliberately let someone see an unglamorous number. Mention the real price of something ordinary — "ugh, groceries were rough this week" — to someone whose opinion you'd normally manage carefully. Small, low-stakes exposure is how you rebuild tolerance for being seen accurately, the same way you'd rebuild any avoided thing: not by fixing it all at once, but by proving, repeatedly, in small doses, that the world doesn't end when the front comes down.

One last thing worth remembering as you practice these overrides: the people worth keeping in your life are, almost without exception, more relieved than judgmental when the mask comes down a little. Most people are quietly performing some version of the same front, worried about the same exposure, and a moment of real honesty from one person at the table tends to give everyone else permission to loosen their own grip slightly, even if only internally. You are rarely the only performer in the room. You're just the one, this time, choosing to stop first.

The mask doesn't protect the person underneath it. It just makes sure no one ever finds out there's a person under there worth protecting honestly instead.

Chapter 7 — The Story That Explains Everything

Why You'd Rather Be Certain Than Wrong About Yourself

She's thirty-four, works in a field she's genuinely good at, has been told so by supervisors more than once in language specific enough that she can't fully dismiss it as politeness. None of that professional competence has ever quite made the crossing into how she feels about her own finances, which she still, some fifteen years into full financial independence, discusses with the faint apologetic energy of someone explaining a chronic and slightly embarrassing condition.

The refund landed on a Tuesday, forty-one dollars more than she'd expected, and for about six seconds it felt like winning something. Then the feeling curdled. She'd forgotten about a bill — an actual, real bill, sitting unpaid in a browser tab she'd closed without looking at — and the refund happened to cover it with room to spare. Lucky. That was the word she reached for. Lucky, not competent. She didn't open her banking app to see why the refund had come through, didn't trace it back to the return she'd made three weeks earlier, didn't let herself register that this was, in fact, a system working the way systems are supposed to work: money going out, money coming back, a ledger balancing itself because she'd taken a reasonable action and the reasonable action had a reasonable consequence. She closed the tab. She thought, *I really do need to get better with money,* and felt, underneath the thought, something closer to relief than shame.

There's a specific tell in how quickly the word arrived, worth noticing on its own. Not "let me check what this is," not even a beat of genuine curiosity about where the extra forty-one dollars came from — just the immediate, reflexive "lucky," arriving before any actual investigation had time to happen. That speed is itself informative. Genuine explanations, ones actually built from evidence, usually take at least a moment to assemble. Explanations built to protect an existing story arrive instantly, because they don't need to gather anything — the conclusion was already decided before the question was even fully asked.

If you'd asked her, in that moment, to walk through what actually happened — step by step, the return, the confirmation email, the processing window, the refund landing exactly when refunds are supposed to land — she could have done it. She wasn't confused about the mechanics. She fully understood that this was cause and effect, her action and its predictable consequence, not a coin flip that happened to land her way. The understanding just wasn't allowed to matter. It sat right next to the "lucky" story, fully formed, fully accurate, and got outvoted anyway, because the story wasn't competing on the merits. It was competing on which version of events let her stop thinking about it fastest, and "lucky" always wins that particular race, because "lucky" requires nothing further of her. Competence would have required an update.

That's the part worth sitting with. Relief.

There's a particular kind of quiet that follows a moment like this, worth describing precisely. Not distress, not even discomfort exactly — something closer to a settling, a small internal exhale, the specific relief of a familiar story reasserting itself after a brief, disorienting wobble. For those six seconds when the refund first registered as good news, something in her had to hold open the possibility that she might be more capable than she believed. That openness is uncomfortable in its own right, even when what it's opening toward is good. Closing it back down, filing the evidence as luck, wasn't just an avoidance of pride. It was a return to familiar ground, and familiar ground, however uncomfortable, is almost always more restful than unfamiliar ground, even good unfamiliar ground.

It's worth noticing, too, how quickly and smoothly "lucky" arrived, compared to how much slower and more effortful the accurate explanation would have been. Luck is a one-word story. It requires no further processing, no revision to anything she believes, no uncomfortable second look at her own competence. The accurate story — I returned something correctly, on time, and the system worked as designed — requires actually crediting herself, however modestly, and crediting yourself is a muscle that atrophies fast in someone who's spent years assuming the credit belongs elsewhere. The word "lucky" wasn't a lie exactly. It was the path of least resistance dressed up as an explanation.

Notice, too, what the relief is specifically attached to — not the extra forty-one dollars itself, but the permission the word "luck" gives her to stop investigating. If she'd let herself trace the refund back to its actual cause, the return she'd handled correctly three weeks earlier, she'd have been forced into a much more demanding kind of attention: reviewing what she'd actually done, noticing it had gone well, updating a self-assessment that's been running on old data for years. That's a lot of cognitive and emotional work for a Tuesday afternoon. "Lucky" short-circuits all of it in one word. It's not just a misattribution. It's an exit ramp, taken instinctively, away from a piece of work that would have been genuinely useful and genuinely uncomfortable in roughly equal measure.

Because if the refund was luck, then the forgotten bill was still the real story — the one where she's bad with money, the one she's told herself, in one form or another, since she was maybe nineteen. And a small, unglamorous financial win didn't fit that story. So rather than let the evidence in, she filed it under an exception. Luck isn't information. Luck doesn't ask you to revise anything. It's the safest possible place to put a fact you don't want to metabolize.

A twenty-nine-year-old runs the same filing system on a much smaller and more painful evidence set. She grew up being told, directly and often, that she was "the creative one, not the money one" — a label assigned in childhood, probably meant kindly, that has quietly organized her entire adult relationship with finances ever since. When she successfully negotiates a raise, using a script she rehearsed for a week and delivered with real skill, she tells the story afterward as "I got lucky, they were probably already planning to give raises." When, a year later, she misses a payment because she genuinely misread a due date on an unusually formatted bill, she tells that story as confirmation — "see, this is exactly why I'm not the money one, I never should have thought I could handle this stuff." Identical categories of event, wildly different evidentiary treatment, and the asymmetry has nothing to do with the events themselves. It has to do with which story was already installed, and installed early enough — before she had any real financial experience of her own to test it against — that it got to define the terms on which all future evidence would be judged, rather than being defined by the evidence itself.

A man in his forties runs the identical filing system in the opposite direction. He's the one in his friend group who's "good with money" — has been for twenty years, ever since he paid off a car loan early in his twenties and told the story enough times that it calcified into an identity. So when an investment he made without much research loses a meaningful chunk of its value, he doesn't file it as "I made a decision that didn't work out," which is what actually happened. He files it as "the market was rigged," or "my broker gave me bad information," or some other externally located explanation that keeps the "good with money" story fully intact. He isn't lying, exactly — he genuinely believes the explanation he lands on. That's what makes the mechanism worth naming: the story doesn't just discount evidence that contradicts it. It actively recruits alternative explanations that leave it standing, and it does this so smoothly the person inside it never experiences it as motivated reasoning. It just feels like accurately assessing what happened.

What's actually happening

There's a name for what she just did, and it isn't denial, exactly — denial implies she didn't see the refund. She saw it.

She used it. She just didn't let it mean anything.

The legal scholar Dan Kahan has spent years studying what he calls identity-protective cognition — the tendency for people to process factual information in ways that defend an identity they've already committed to, rather than in ways that arrive at the most accurate belief. His research grew out of political and scientific topics — climate change, vaccines, gun policy — where he found something strange: giving people more information, better data, clearer facts, didn't reliably change their minds. In some cases it made their positions more entrenched, because the information was being run through a filter that asked not "is this true?" but "what does believing this cost me, and who would I have to become if I accepted it?"

Money works on the same filter. Most people don't hold a neutral, evolving theory of their own financial competence that updates cleanly every time new evidence arrives. They hold a *story* — "I'm bad with money," "I'm the responsible one," "I'm just not a numbers person," "I always land on my feet" — and the story was usually installed early, often by a single vivid memory or a repeated family verdict, and it has been quietly running the show ever since. The story isn't neutral. It's load-bearing. It explains past failures, sets expectations for future ones, and — this is the part that matters — it lets a person stop investigating themselves, because the case is already closed.

Kahan's work also documented something that should make anyone pause before assuming self-awareness is a cure: he found that people who scored higher on measures of numeracy and analytical skill weren't more resistant to identity-protective reasoning — they were often more effective at it. A person with strong reasoning skills doesn't lose the ability to filter evidence through identity; they simply build more sophisticated, more persuasive-sounding rationalizations for the filtering. "I'm not avoiding this, I'm being appropriately skeptical of a fluke result" sounds like careful thinking. It can also be, simultaneously, a beautifully constructed wall. The tools that would seem best equipped to overcome the filter — intelligence, analytical training, a genuine desire to be accurate — turn out to be just as available to the filter's defense as to its dismantling. This is why so much financial self-awareness work fails: it assumes the problem is a lack of good reasoning, when the actual problem is that good reasoning has been recruited to serve a story that was never chosen consciously in the first place.

An unexpected refund doesn't just sit there as a data point. It shows up as a *threat*, because it contradicts the verdict. If she's bad with money, and the refund proves a moment of financial competence — remembering to return something, doing it correctly, having the system respond exactly as designed — then the verdict is wrong. And if the verdict is wrong, she has to ask a much harder question than "was that lucky?" She has to ask: *if I'm not actually bad with money, then what have I been protecting myself from by believing I was?* That question doesn't have a six-second answer. Luck does. So luck wins, every time, unless something interrupts the reflex.

This is why the identity story survives contact with contradicting evidence so easily. It isn't stupidity and it isn't laziness. It's a defense that's doing exactly what defenses do — protecting something that feels more urgent to protect than accuracy. Kahan's research suggests this reflex gets stronger, not weaker, in people who are otherwise sharp and numerically capable, because sharper reasoning just means a more sophisticated filing system for the evidence you don't want to keep.

It's worth being precise about what this means for how you evaluate your own thinking going forward. The presence of a confident, well-reasoned explanation for a financial outcome is not, on its own, evidence that the explanation is accurate — it might just be evidence that your identity had a strong incentive to produce a confident, well-reasoned explanation in that particular direction. This doesn't mean you should distrust every conclusion you reach about your own finances. It means the conclusions worth double-checking most carefully are precisely the ones that arrive fastest, feel most obviously true, and happen to leave your existing self-image completely undisturbed. Those are the conclusions most likely to have been produced by the filter rather than by the facts.

The psychologists Jennifer Crocker and Connie Wolfe, who study contingencies of self-worth, add a piece that explains why some people's stories are more brittle than others. Their research found that when self-esteem is heavily staked on a specific domain — being "the smart one," "the responsible one," "the good-with-money one" — evidence in that domain gets processed with far more emotional intensity and far more defensive filtering than evidence in domains the person doesn't stake their worth on. The man with the twenty-year-old car-loan story isn't just protecting a preference. He's protecting the specific plank his self-esteem stands on, which is exactly why a single bad investment produces an outsized defensive reaction rather than a shrug. If money weren't load-bearing for his sense of worth, the loss would just be a loss. Because it is load-bearing, the loss has to be someone else's fault, or the whole structure wobbles.

What it costs you

The money cost is the easier one to name. A person who reflexively discounts evidence of their own competence never builds a track record they trust, which means they never graduate to slightly bigger, slightly bolder financial decisions — negotiating a rate, questioning a fee, investing a windfall instead of parking it out of fear they'll "mess it up." The story keeps them small in ways that compound. Somebody who believes

"I'm bad with money" doesn't apply for the raise, doesn't read the offer letter closely, doesn't ask what the fee actually covers, because asking implies a person capable of understanding the answer, and that's not the story. Every year the story stays unexamined is a year of decisions made by the story instead of by the numbers.

This shows up most starkly at decision points that only come around rarely — a job offer, an inheritance, a first real opportunity to invest meaningfully — because rare decisions don't get the benefit of practice. A person with an unexamined "not good with money" story tends to hand these moments off entirely, to a partner, a parent, whoever in their orbit is willing to take the decision on, not because that person is necessarily better equipped, but because handing it off feels safer than making a decision that might expose the story as either true or false. Ironically, this handoff behavior often produces exactly the outcome the story predicted — a person who never makes financial decisions never gets the experience of making good ones, which means the story gets to remain permanently unfalsified, protected not by evidence but by its own refusal to be tested.

The quieter cost is what it does to her relationship with herself. Somewhere underneath "I'm bad with money" is usually an older sentence — "I'm careless," "I'm not someone people can rely on," "I don't deserve for things to go well for me" — and every time she discounts a win as luck, she isn't just misreading a bank statement. She's reconfirming the older sentence. She's telling herself, again, in a language so quiet she doesn't register it as a decision: *the good version of me isn't the real one.* That's a heavier tax than any bank fee. It's the tax of never getting to fully believe good evidence about your own life, because good evidence keeps arriving in a currency your identity has already decided not to accept.

And it isolates her, in a specific way. She can't ask for help managing money she's decided she's incapable of managing "for real" — that would mean admitting the story to someone else, which risks someone else disagreeing with it, which is its own kind of threat. So she manages alone, inside a story that was never fact-checked, making decisions engineered to be consistent with a self-image instead of decisions engineered to be good.

There's a longer-arc cost too, one that only becomes visible looking backward over a decade rather than forward from any single moment. A person who has spent ten years discounting their own competence as luck has, by definition, never let themselves accumulate a felt sense of a track record — even if the actual track record, examined honestly, would show a person who mostly gets things right. Ask her how many financial decisions she's made well over the last decade and she genuinely won't know, not because the decisions weren't good, but because good ones got filed as exceptions instead of as data. She's sitting on a decade of quiet evidence for a self she's never been permitted to believe in.

There's a quiet grief buried inside this pattern, worth naming directly rather than just analytically: somewhere she is carrying a version of herself she has genuinely never gotten to meet — the one the honest evidence log would reveal, competent more often than not, reasonably careful, making mostly sound decisions across a decade she's mentally filed as "a mess." That person exists, in the record, whether or not she's ever been permitted to know her. The tragedy isn't the discounted refund. It's the decade of not getting introduced to someone she'd probably like.

This has a specific, practical downstream effect worth naming: people without a felt sense of their own track record tend to seek far more external reassurance than their actual competence warrants, running every decision past a partner, a friend, a forum, an advisor — not because a second opinion is bad practice, but because the seeking has become a substitute for trusting a self-assessment that was never allowed to form. This isn't humility. It looks like humility, and gets praised as humility, but it's actually a symptom of the identity-protective filter operating so thoroughly that the person has lost access to their own evidence base entirely. The fix isn't more external reassurance. It's finally letting the internal ledger get an honest read.

The overrides

One more thing worth knowing before the overrides: the story doesn't just discount good news. It also, perversely, sometimes discounts bad news that would actually prompt useful action, if the bad news doesn't match the story either. Someone whose story is "I always land on my feet" can wave off a genuinely concerning pattern — mounting debt, a retirement account that isn't on track — with the same reflexive dismissal she applies to good evidence, just aimed the other direction. The filter isn't loyal to optimism or pessimism. It's loyal to the existing story, whatever that story happens to be, and it will discount any evidence, in either direction, that threatens to update it. That's why the log below asks you to record both kinds of evidence honestly — not to prove you're secretly great with money, and not to catastrophize either, but to let the actual pattern, whatever it turns out to be, finally get a vote.

Name the filter before you use it. The next time something financial goes better than expected — a refund, a bill lower than budgeted, a bonus, an account that grew — say out loud or write down the first explanation your mind reaches for. If the automatic word is "luck," "fluke," or "they must have made a mistake," stop and ask one question: *what would I have to* *believe about myself if this wasn't luck?* You don't have to answer it fully. Just let the question exist for thirty seconds before you file the win away. That pause is where the filter loses its grip.

The Move: keep a two-column evidence log for thirty days. One column: "things that happened because I was careless." Other column: "things that happened because I did something right, even something small." Every time either kind of event happens — forgot a payment, caught an error, remembered a due date, got a refund — log it in the honest column, not the column your identity prefers. At the end of thirty days, read both columns side by side. Most people expecting a landslide for the "bad with money" column find something closer to a split, sometimes a majority in the other direction. The log doesn't argue with you. It just outvotes the story with things you can't unsee, because you wrote them yourself.

Resist the urge to stop the log early if the first week looks discouraging, and resist the opposite urge to stop it early if the first week looks great. Thirty days is the minimum window for a reason: identity-protective filtering doesn't give up its grip in a week, and a short trial will just get reabsorbed into whichever story was already dominant. The value of the exercise comes specifically from the accumulation — thirty individually unremarkable entries becoming, together, a body of evidence too large and too self-documented for the old filter to wave away with a single "well, that one was luck."

Rehearse being wrong about yourself in public, on purpose. Once, this week, tell one person a piece of financial evidence that contradicts your usual story — "actually, I caught that fee before it hit," "I did the math right on that one" — without the self-deprecating hedge that usually follows it. No "but I'm still bad with this stuff, obviously." Just let the fact stand alone, in front of a witness. This is exposure in miniature: proving, in a low-stakes moment, that a slightly more accurate self-story doesn't collapse anything. It's a rehearsal for the bigger revision that's coming.

One final note before this chapter closes: revising the story doesn't mean swinging to the opposite extreme and deciding you're now, definitively, "great with money" — that's just a new fused identity, as brittle as the old one, equally vulnerable to a single bad month knocking it down. The goal isn't a better story. It's a looser relationship to the idea of having a fixed financial identity at all. Some months will go well. Some won't. Neither needs to be metabolized into a verdict about who you fundamentally are. That flexibility — not a new, nicer label — is the actual destination.

The Rule to Remember: The story was never about whether you're good with money. It was about whether you could survive finding out you might be.

Chapter 8 — The Punishment You Assign Yourself

Why Guilt Spending Feels Like Justice

She overspends on a small indulgence minutes after a stressful collections call, feeling relief instead of alarm. Twenty-three dollars for a candle, a face mask, and a coffee she didn't need — bought with the phone still warm from a call about $340 she doesn't have.

She'd been putting off answering that number for six weeks — not ignoring it entirely, exactly, but managing it the way you manage a low fever, checking in on it occasionally without ever actually treating it, hoping it would resolve on its own if she just gave it enough time. Six unanswered calls from an unfamiliar area code, three voicemails she listened to at 1.5x speed with her thumb already hovering over delete, one letter she genuinely, this time, did open, read halfway, and set aside with the specific promise to herself that she'd "deal with it this weekend." The seventh call, she answered, mostly by reflex, phone already in her hand for an unrelated reason, thumb sliding to accept before her brain fully registered what number was calling.

The scent of the collections agent's voice is still in her ear — polite, procedural, the particular flatness of someone reading from a script that was written to survive being yelled at. She'd said the number out loud back to him, because he asked her to confirm it, and something about saying it in her own voice made it real in a way the letter never had. $340. Overdue. Then a pause where he explained the next steps, and she'd nodded along to a phone call, agreeing to things she'd stopped fully hearing.

She hangs up. Her hands are unsteady in the specific way hands get after a fight that wasn't a fight — too much adrenaline with nowhere to go. She opens her laptop, not to check the number, but to get away from it. A tab is already open to a store she likes. Fifteen minutes later there's a candle in a small paper bag by her door, and — this is the part worth sitting with — she feels *better*. Not distracted-better. Better like something has been settled.

She'll think about this call, on and off, for the rest of the day — replaying the agent's flat, procedural voice, replaying her own voice reading the number back to him, cringing slightly at a stammer she doesn't think he noticed but she can't stop hearing. The candle arrives two days later, and by then the acute panic has faded into something dumber and more diffuse — a general, low-grade dread about money that doesn't have a specific trigger anymore, just a permanent hum underneath the day. She lights the candle anyway. It smells like cedar and something floral she can't place, and for the length of one evening, sitting in that smell, she feels like a person whose life is basically fine. That feeling is real. It's just not about the $340, and it never touches the $340, and tomorrow the $340 will still be exactly $340, plus whatever accrued overnight.

That flicker of relief is the whole chapter. Not the spending. The relief.

Notice, too, the specific choice of purchase — not something practical, not something that addresses the actual $340, but something small, sensory, self-soothing, chosen almost entirely for how it will make the next twenty minutes feel rather than for any lasting value. That's not incidental. The nervous system, mid-shame-spike, isn't shopping for utility. It's shopping for a fast, reliable dose of a specific feeling, and candles, treats, small indulgent purchases are extremely good at delivering exactly that feeling, exactly that fast — which is precisely why they're so easy to reach for and so hard, in the moment, to talk yourself out of.

If you asked her, a week from now, to explain the candle purchase, she'd probably laugh a little, call it a small treat, a moment of self-care after a rough day — a story that's true in the loosest possible sense and completely misses what actually happened in her body in that fifteen-minute window. The story she'll tell later is retrofitted, assembled after the fact to make a reflexive, shame-driven purchase sound like a deliberate, healthy choice. That's not dishonesty. It's just how quickly the mind builds a plausible narrative around something it did for reasons it never consciously examined.

A father of two, forty-one, runs the identical mechanism at a scale with much higher real stakes. He's just had a hard conversation with his wife about the state of a joint credit card he'd been managing without full transparency — not deception exactly, more a slow accumulation of small omissions, each individually defensible, that had compounded into a number neither of them had fully seen until that evening. The conversation was difficult but not cruel; she was more worried than angry. He leaves the house afterward, ostensibly to "clear his head," and comes back two hours later having bought his kids a genuinely lavish amount of takeout and a movie neither of them had asked for, presenting it as a spontaneous, generous surprise. His kids are delighted. His wife recognizes, without being able to fully articulate it in the moment, that something about the gesture doesn't sit right, that it arrived one hour too fast after a hard conversation to be simple generosity. What he's actually doing, without any conscious plan to do it, is trying to buy back, in a single grand gesture, the version of himself as a good provider that the credit card conversation had just badly dented. The kids get a fun night. The actual problem — the transparency, the number, the pattern of small omissions — goes completely unaddressed, buried under a receipt for a night that felt, to him, like redemption.

A college student, twenty, runs the identical mechanism at a scale that matters just as much to him even though the numbers are smaller. He checks his account after a night out he can't quite remember spending on, sees a number lower than he expected, and the shame-spike arrives right on schedule — that specific hot, sinking feeling of having disappointed a version of himself he was trying to be this semester, the responsible one, the one who wasn't going to repeat his freshman-year overdraft habit. Twenty minutes later he's ordered food he didn't need, on a card that's already the problem, because the ordering itself — the tap, the confirmation screen, the "arriving in 25 minutes" — produces an immediate, physical sense of agency that directly counters the helplessness of the shame spike. It isn't hunger. It's a demonstration to himself, staged in real time, that he still gets to make choices, even though the choice he's making is the exact one making things worse.

What's actually happening

Picture someone watching this from the outside — a coworker who happened to be nearby during the call, who then watches her open a laptop and order a candle fifteen minutes later. From that vantage point, the sequence looks almost willfully self-destructive, the kind of thing that invites an eye-roll or a quiet, judgmental "well, that explains a lot." That outside read is exactly what makes moral judgments about spending so unhelpful and so common — they evaluate the behavior with none of the internal context that actually produced it, and the behavior, stripped of context, looks like carelessness instead of what it actually is: a nervous system doing the only thing it currently knows how to do with an overwhelming feeling.

The instinct is to read this as a contradiction: how does someone who just felt the floor drop out from under her finances respond by spending more? It looks like the opposite of a lesson learned. But it isn't a contradiction once you understand what the purchase is actually doing. It isn't consumption. It's punctuation.

If you asked her, immediately after the purchase, whether the candle was a good financial decision, she'd say no without hesitation — she's not confused about the arithmetic. She could tell you, accurately and immediately, that twenty-three dollars against a $340 balance moves her further from solvent, not closer. The confusion isn't factual. It's that the purchase was never trying to answer a factual question. It was answering an emotional one — *can I still do something, can I still choose, am I still a person with agency in this moment* — and against that question, twenty-three dollars for a candle is, by its own internal logic, a resounding, immediate yes. Two completely different accounting systems were running at once, and only one of them got consulted before her hand moved.

Researchers who study guilt and consumer behavior — including work by Dilip Soman on how people mentally account for spending, and a broader line of behavioral-economics research on what's often called moral licensing — have documented a pattern that shows up across very different contexts: people who feel they've done something wrong often don't retreat from further action. They take an action that lets them *close the account.* A small purchase after a moment of financial shame isn't usually experienced, in the moment, as more damage. It's experienced as a full stop at the end of a sentence that was starting to spiral.

Here's the mechanism in plain terms. Shame is not a data point. It's a state — a flood of feeling that says something about *you*, not something about a number on a page. The call didn't just deliver information ("you owe $340"). It delivered an indictment ("you are the kind of person this happens to"). And an indictment demands a verdict. The mind wants the feeling to resolve, wants a moment where it can say: *there. Handled.* A twenty-dollar candle can't touch $340. But it can absolutely deliver the emotional experience of "I did something. I took an action. I am back in control." The purchase isn't paying off the debt. It's paying off the shame — or trying to. It's a receipt for a different transaction entirely, one that has nothing to do with money and everything to do with proving, quickly, to yourself, that you still get to make choices.

The psychologist Richard Lazarus, whose work on stress and coping shaped much of how the field still thinks about emotional regulation, drew a distinction that clarifies exactly what's happening in that fifteen-minute window: problem-focused coping, which changes the actual situation causing distress, versus emotion-focused coping, which changes how the distress feels without touching its source. Both are legitimate, useful strategies — Lazarus was clear that emotion-focused coping isn't inherently worse, and sometimes it's the only available option when a situation genuinely can't be changed in the moment. The trouble isn't that she reached for emotion-focused coping after the call. A hot shower, a walk, a call to a friend — any of those would have done the identical emotional job without opening her wallet. The trouble is that the specific emotion-focused strategy she reached for was one that actively worsens the problem-focused situation underneath it. She didn't just fail to fix the $340. She added to it, while her nervous system quietly filed the whole sequence under "handled."

There's a second layer under that, and it's the more interesting one. Some of what's happening is closer to self-punishment than to relief-seeking. The candle isn't only a reset — it's occasionally a small penance, a version of "well, I'm already the kind of person who's bad with money, so." Once the identity has been assigned — irresponsible, behind, a person collections agencies call — a small indulgent purchase doesn't feel like it's violating that identity. It feels like it's *consistent* with it. You don't protect a budget you don't believe belongs to a competent person. The story writes the behavior, not the other way around.

This is a specific and underappreciated trap. Once shame has assigned you a role, behavior that confirms the role can feel, perversely, more comfortable than behavior that contradicts it. That's true even when the contradicting behavior would objectively serve you better. Saving the twenty-three dollars instead of spending it would be the "responsible" move, but responsible isn't the role currently assigned to her, and acting outside your assigned role produces its own kind of dissonance, however small. Spending it, on the other hand, requires nothing new of her. It simply continues the story that's already running, and continuing a familiar story, even an unflattering one, is almost always easier than the unfamiliar work of writing a different one.

This is the master pattern this book keeps returning to: the numbers were never really about the numbers. They were about who you'd have to admit you are if you looked at them squarely. The collections call forced a look. The candle was the fastest available way to look away again — not by refusing to see the number, but by immediately generating a new feeling loud enough to drown the old one out.

What it costs you

The money cost is the easy one to name and the least important. Twenty-three dollars against a $340 balance is not what sinks anyone. It's the *pattern* of twenty-three dollars, repeated every time a stressful money moment produces a stress-relieving purchase, that compounds into something real — a second, invisible expense category running parallel to the actual bills, funded entirely by shame and paid for with money that was needed elsewhere.

If you actually totaled this category across a year for someone running this pattern regularly — every collections call, every uncomfortable balance check, every moment of financial dread met with a small counter-purchase — the number is often genuinely startling, not because any single purchase was large, but because the triggers are so frequent for someone under real financial pressure. That's the cruel design of the loop: the people most likely to have frequent shame spikes are, almost by definition, the people who can least afford a parallel expense category running underneath their actual budget. The mechanism doesn't spare the people who most need it to. If anything, it targets them hardest, because a stressed financial life produces more triggering moments, and more triggering moments produce more twenty-three-dollar candles, in a loop that has no natural ceiling unless something interrupts it deliberately.

But the quieter cost is the one worth slowing down for. Every time a purchase successfully resolves the *feeling* of the money problem without touching the money problem itself, it teaches the nervous system that this is what resolution feels like. The brain doesn't naturally distinguish between "I fixed something" and "I felt like I fixed something" — both register as relief, both get reinforced, both get reached for again next time. Over months, this builds a person who has a highly practiced, well-worn path from *financial fear* to *small purchase* to *temporary calm*, and almost no practiced path from *financial fear* to *looking at the actual number* to *earned calm*. The skill that atrophies isn't budgeting. It's tolerance — the simple, learnable capacity to sit inside an uncomfortable fact for longer than four minutes without needing to do something to make the feeling stop.

And there's an identity cost that's easy to miss because it doesn't announce itself. Each of these purchases is a small vote for the story that you're someone who can't hold financial stress without needing a release valve. It's not that anyone consciously thinks this. It's that the behavior, repeated, becomes the evidence — and evidence, unlike opinion, is hard to argue yourself out of later. The candle isn't just twenty-three dollars. It's a ballot cast for a version of yourself you didn't mean to vote for.

There's a compounding version of this cost that shows up specifically at the next shame spike, and the one after that. Once the fear-purchase-relief loop has run a few times, the mind starts anticipating it — meaning the next hard money moment doesn't just produce shame, it produces shame *plus* a faint, automatic pull toward the exact behavior that will resolve it fastest. The loop gets more efficient with practice, the way any well-rehearsed sequence does. That efficiency is the opposite of what you want. You're not just spending twenty-three dollars periodically. You're sanding down the path between distress and spending until it takes almost no resistance to walk it.

There's a version of this student worth naming too, a mirror of the twenty-year-old from earlier in this chapter but a decade further along: a thirty-year-old professional who has upgraded her coping purchase from food delivery to something more sophisticated-sounding — a "self-care Sunday" spending ritual she's built an entire aesthetic vocabulary around, candles and skincare and a particular brand of tea, framed to herself and to her social media followers as wellness rather than what it functionally is, which is the identical mechanism from Chapter 8 wearing a more expensive, more socially acceptable costume. The dressing changes with income and age. The underlying transaction — buying a feeling instead of addressing a fact — stays exactly the same.

There's a final layer worth naming: the loop also quietly trains the people around you, if they're paying attention, to associate your hard money moments with a very specific, very readable tell — the small treat, the "spontaneous" purchase, the sudden and slightly forced cheerfulness that shows up right after a stressful call. A perceptive partner or close friend may start to recognize the pattern before you do, which can produce its own strange shame spiral: now you're not just managing the original financial stress, you're managing the fact that your coping mechanism has become visible, has a name in someone else's head even if it doesn't yet have one in yours. Naming it yourself, first, on your own terms, is almost always less costly than having someone else name it for you.

The overrides

Before the overrides, it's worth naming the goal precisely, because it's easy to misread this chapter as "never buy anything to feel better," which isn't the point and isn't realistic. Comfort purchases aren't the enemy. Plenty of people buy themselves a small, deliberate treat after a hard day and it's a healthy, proportionate act of self-care that costs them nothing they can't afford and helps them regulate a genuinely hard moment. The problem isn't the candle. It's the *automaticity* — the purchase happening before any conscious choice gets to weigh in, triggered by shame specifically, aimed at numbing a feeling rather than actually choosing a comfort. The goal of what follows isn't austerity. It's putting a few seconds of daylight between the trigger and the transaction, so that if you do decide to buy the candle, it's a decision you made, not a reflex that made itself.

The Move: build a four-minute bridge. The specific danger window is the fifteen or so minutes right after a shame spike — a call, a notification, an unopened bill you finally opened. In that window, install one deliberate delay: before any purchase over a small set threshold you pick in advance (even ten dollars), you have to do one unrelated four-minute task first — walk to the end of the block and back, write down the number you just heard in a notes app, text one friend the sentence "just had a hard money call." The task doesn't need to be productive. It only needs to occupy the same four minutes the impulse purchase would have occupied, so the urge has to survive contact with a small delay instead of being acted on instantly. Most guilt purchases are made inside a five-minute window of peak feeling; interrupt the window and the urge frequently just — passes.

Name the transaction out loud. When you catch the impulse rising, say to yourself, specifically: "I'm not buying this because I want it. I'm buying it to stop feeling like I just got in trouble." You don't have to talk yourself out of the purchase. You just have to make the real transaction visible before it happens. It's much harder to spend money on a feeling once you've said out loud what the feeling actually is — the sentence itself does a lot of the work the willpower can't.

Separate the apology from the correction. After a shame-spike moment, give yourself permission to do something small and kind that has nothing to do with money at all — a hot shower, ten minutes outside, a text to someone who'll say something reassuring. Let that be the reset. Then, separately, later, with a calmer nervous system, do the actual correction: look at the number again, even for sixty seconds, even without deciding anything. This breaks the fused habit of *feeling better* and *spending money* being the same motion — and it starts building the other path, the one where relief comes from looking rather than looking away.

Keep a running list of two or three non-spending resets that genuinely work for you specifically, and keep it somewhere accessible — written down, not just remembered, because in the fifteen-minute window right after a shame spike, memory is exactly the faculty under the most strain. A list you can glance at removes the need to improvise a solution while already flooded, which is asking too much of yourself in the hardest possible moment. The goal isn't willpower in the heat of the spike. It's removing the need for willpower by having the better option already queued up and ready before the spike ever arrives.

One last thought before moving to the final chapter: the goal here isn't to eliminate every comfort purchase forever, or to treat every treat as suspect. It's to build enough of a pause between a shame spike and a purchase that you get to choose, rather than react — and sometimes, having paused, you'll choose the candle anyway, deliberately, with full awareness of what it is and isn't doing for you. That's completely different from buying it on autopilot in the first ninety seconds after a hard phone call. The four-minute bridge isn't a ban. It's a chance to actually decide.

The Rule to Remember: The candle was never the crime. It was a sentence you handed yourself — and you're allowed to close the case without paying a fine you didn't actually owe.

Chapter 9 — The Number That Isn't You

Why Separating the Fact From the Feeling Changes What You Do Next

It's a Thursday evening in early autumn, nothing about the day distinguishing it from any other, which is itself worth noting — the moments that end up mattering most in a long process of change rarely announce themselves as significant while they're happening. You'd half expected, somewhere in the back of your mind, that whenever this finally shifted, it would shift on a dramatic day, a day that had earned it. Instead it's an ordinary Thursday, dishes still in the sink, a show paused on the television in the other room.

You opened the account before you'd decided to. That was the strange part — no pep talk, no bracing, just the mouse moving toward the button the way your hand moves toward a doorknob you've touched ten thousand times. The page loaded. The balance sat there, plain: $340.12.

It's worth noticing what's different about tonight, because the difference is the entire lesson of this final chapter compressed into a single evening. You've opened this exact account a hundred times before, under a hundred different versions of dread, and every one of those times the number arrived pre-loaded with a verdict already stapled to it. Tonight, for reasons that aren't fully clear even to you, the staple didn't hold. Maybe it was the specific week you'd had. Maybe it was simply the accumulated weight of every small override you'd practiced across every chapter before this one, each one wearing down the fusion a little further without your fully noticing the wear. Whatever the cause, tonight the number arrived alone, unaccompanied, and that's the whole difference between every previous time you've opened this account and this one.

This is the same account from a few chapters back — the one with the collections call, the twenty-three-dollar candle, the four-minute bridge you've been practicing since. Tonight there's no shame spike triggering this check, no dread built up over days. It's just Thursday, your usual day now, the standing appointment you set weeks ago and have mostly kept since. You almost didn't notice yourself opening the app. That's new too.

There's a detail worth noting about the physical setting, small but telling: you're sitting, not standing, and the posture matters more than it seems like it should. Standing is a posture your body associates with bracing, with readiness to move away from something. Sitting, settled into a chair with the laptop resting on your legs, is a posture your body associates with safety, with staying put. You didn't choose the posture deliberately to signal safety to your own nervous system. But it's doing that work anyway, quietly, underneath the actual content of what's on the screen.

You read it out loud. Not dramatically. The way a pilot reads back an altitude, the way someone reads a thermometer. "Three hundred forty dollars and twelve cents." Your own voice sounded strange saying it, flat and unimpressive, like reading a grocery list.

There's a small, specific piece of muscle memory worth naming here: your jaw, which has clenched at this exact moment in this exact app more times than you could count, stayed loose. Your shoulders, which usually climb toward your ears the instant a balance resolves into digits, stayed where they were.

These aren't symbolic details. They're the actual, physical site where all the previous chapters' work has been quietly accumulating — not in your thoughts, primarily, but in your body's rehearsed response to a stimulus it has been slowly, patiently retrained to meet differently.

And then you waited for the thing that always came next. The tightening. The heat behind your sternum. The voice that says *this is what you are.* You waited for it the way you'd wait for a stair you know is missing.

It didn't come. Or it came, but smaller — a flicker, there and gone, like a shadow passing over a wall instead of the wall catching fire. You were still you. The dog still needed walking. The coffee was still too hot to drink. Nothing about the actual shape of your life had shifted in the four seconds since you'd read the number. You were exactly as capable, exactly as loved, exactly as far along as you'd been thirty seconds earlier, back when the number was still hidden and your chest was still tight with the *idea* of it.

There's something worth naming about the specific number itself, separate from the fusion mechanism entirely: $340.12 is, by any reasonable external measure, a manageable figure — not nothing, not comfortable, but survivable, workable, the kind of number that a calm, unhurried Thursday can absorb without much drama. It took this many chapters and this much practice to let a perfectly manageable number simply be read as a manageable number. That's worth sitting with on its own, independent of any larger lesson: the actual math was never the hard part. It rarely is.

This is the moment the rest of the book has been walking you toward, and it's smaller than you expected. Not a triumph. Not a breakthrough set to music. Just a number, sitting in a sentence, not attached to anything.

You sit with that for a minute, almost suspicious of how little happened. Some part of you expected more — expected that finally looking, after however many years of flinching, would produce something dramatic, a release, a cathartic exhale, the kind of moment a movie would score with strings. It didn't. It produced almost nothing at all, which is its own kind of strange gift, because "almost nothing" is precisely what a number is supposed to produce. The years of dread had built you up for an earthquake. What you got was a Tuesday.

A twenty-five-year-old reaches a smaller-scale version of the same moment on her own, with no advisor in the room, just a spreadsheet she finally forces herself to build after a year of guessing. She's expecting the finished total — student loans, a car payment, a stubborn credit card balance from a rough stretch after graduation — to be catastrophic, a number that will confirm every fear she's carried since she started avoiding this exact spreadsheet. When it's finished, the number is bad. It is not, however, the number she'd built up in her head; it's smaller, more specific, more actionable than the shapeless dread that preceded it. She sits with that for a long moment, not celebrating, because the debt is real and the road ahead is real — but noticing, distinctly, that the finished fact takes up less room in her chest than the unfinished fear did. The dread had no edges. The number has edges. Edges, it turns out, are something you can actually work with.

A father in his late thirties reaches the same moment from a harder angle. He's sitting across from a financial advisor, at his wife's insistence, going through a debt consolidation plan he's dreaded discussing for over a year — credit cards from a stretch of unemployment neither of them talks about directly anymore. The advisor reads the total balance out loud, flatly, the way advisors are trained to, no inflection, no judgment in the voice at all — just a number in a sentence, the same weather-report register the rest of this chapter has been building toward. And he notices, almost with surprise, that hearing someone *else* say it in that flat register does something his own inner voice never could: it makes the number sound like what it actually is, a fact being reported, rather than what his own head always turned it into, a sentence being handed down. Sometimes defusion doesn't come from inside you at all. Sometimes it takes a second person's calm, factual voice to model what your own voice has never once managed to do with this particular number.

What's actually happening

For your whole financial life, one particular sleight of hand has been running underneath everything: the number and the verdict have been fused into a single object. "$340 in checking" was never allowed to just be $340 in checking. It arrived pre-loaded with a second sentence stapled to its back — *you're behind, you're careless, you're the reason this family struggles, you're not a real adult yet* — and because those two sentences arrived together, at the same instant, in the same breath, your mind stopped being able to tell them apart. The fact and the verdict became one fused thing. Look at the fact, and you take the verdict full in the chest, every time, no exceptions.

The psychologist Steven Hayes developed Acceptance and Commitment Therapy, and he has a name for the mechanism that fuses them: *cognitive fusion.* It's the mind's habit of treating a thought as identical to the reality it's describing, rather than as one perspective on it. A piece of language that could be examined rather than obeyed. When you're fused with a thought, you don't have the thought. The thought has you. "I have $340" and "I am a failure" stop being two separate claims — one checkable against a bank statement, one a sweeping character verdict with no evidence bar at all — and become a single, seamless experience: *number equals doom.*

The antidote Hayes and others in that tradition developed is called *defusion* — not arguing with the thought, not disproving it, not replacing it with a nicer one, but simply putting a few inches of daylight between yourself and it. Between the thought and the thinker. You did this by accident tonight, and it's worth naming exactly what you did, because it's repeatable.

Hayes was explicit about something counterintuitive that matters here: defusion doesn't work by fighting the thought or proving it wrong. Trying to argue yourself out of "I'm bad with money" usually backfires, because arguing keeps you fused to the thought — you're still standing inside its frame, just contesting the verdict from within the same courtroom. Defusion works by changing your *relationship* to the thought instead, stepping outside the courtroom altogether. You're not claiming the thought is false. You're noticing that it's a thought — a mental event, with a beginning and an end, that arose and will pass — rather than a fact fused permanently to your identity. This is a smaller ask than "believe something different about yourself," which is why it works more often than positive-thinking approaches that demand you argue yourself into an opposite, equally unverified belief. You don't have to believe you're good with money. You just have to notice that "I'm bad with money" is a sentence your mind produces, not a law of physics governing who you are.

You read the number out loud, in a flat, factual register — the weather-report voice, not the confession voice. That single move does something specific: it converts an *internal, fused, identity-level event* ("I am the kind of person who only has $340") into an *external, spoken, fact-level event* ("the balance is three hundred forty dollars and twelve cents"). Saying a thing in a plain factual sentence forces your mind to process it as data for half a second before the old story can grab it. That half-second is the whole trick. It's not that the shame disappears — it's that it arrives a beat late, and in that beat, you get to notice: *this is a number. That was a story. They are not the same object.*

There's a reason speaking the number out loud works better than simply thinking it, and it has to do with how differently the mind processes internal and externalized language. A thought that stays entirely internal moves fast, tangled up with feeling, hard to separate from the emotional response accompanying it.

The moment you convert that same thought into spoken words — actual sound, actual breath, actual muscles moving in your mouth and throat — you've forced it through a slower, more deliberate channel that naturally creates distance between the thing being said and the self doing the saying. This is part of why people talk to themselves out loud when trying to think clearly under pressure, why coaches tell athletes to narrate their own actions, why "just say it out loud" turns out to be genuinely good advice rather than a folk saying. Speech is slower than thought, and slower, here, is exactly the point.

This is also, not incidentally, exactly the move the book's central claim has been circling from the first chapter: the numbers you refuse to look at were never really about the numbers. They were about who you'd have to admit you are if you looked. Defusion doesn't fix your finances. It does something arguably more load-bearing first — it proves, in your own nervous system, that looking doesn't cost you your identity. Once that's proven even once, the whole architecture of avoidance loses its foundation. There's nothing left to flinch from except a number, and numbers, it turns out, are almost boring.

What it costs you

The financial cost of fusion is the one you can already list, because you've been living it for chapters: the late fees on autopilot, the balance transfer never explored because exploring it meant reading it, the retirement contribution set at the bare minimum because raising it meant opening a screen you couldn't stand to look at. Avoidance is expensive, and it compounds, silently, in the exact places you've stopped checking.

It's worth pausing on the word "compounds" here, because it's doing more than rhetorical work. Financial neglect behaves mathematically the same way financial growth does — small, unaddressed gaps widen over time through the same exponential logic that makes early retirement contributions so much more powerful than late ones. A fee left unquestioned for one year is a minor annoyance. The same fee left unquestioned for a decade, plus every other small unexamined leak accumulated alongside it, is a genuinely large sum, not because any single decision was catastrophic, but because avoidance, uniquely among financial mistakes, doesn't announce its own size. A bad investment shows you a number. Neglect just shows you nothing at all, for years, until the eventual reckoning arrives all at once and gets misread — one more time — as evidence that you were bad with money all along, when what actually happened was a long accumulation of small, compounding absences.

But the quieter cost is the one that matters more, because it's the one that never shows up on a statement. Every time the number and the verdict fuse, you don't just avoid a fact — you rehearse a self. You practice, one more time, being the person who can't look. And selves built out of rehearsal get stronger with repetition, the same way any habit does. The avoidance isn't just protecting you from a bad feeling in the moment. It's laying down track. Ten years of not-looking doesn't leave you exactly where you started; it leaves you as someone for whom not-looking has become load-bearing, structural, part of how you hold yourself together. That's a much larger thing to lose than a late fee. It's the version of you that gets to feel, even once, *capable in the presence of your own facts.* Fusion doesn't just cost money. It costs you the experience of finding out you might be fine.

There's a final cost worth naming, because it's the one this whole book has been building toward undoing: fusion doesn't stay contained to money. Someone who has spent years treating a bank balance as a character verdict tends to run the same fusion on other numbers too — the scale, the performance review score, the follower count, the standardized test result their kid brought home. The mechanism doesn't know it's supposed to be about money specifically. It's a general-purpose habit of collapsing measurement into meaning, and once you've built it strong enough in one domain, it tends to show up, uninvited, in most of the others. Which is also, in a way, good news. Learn to defuse it here, with a bank balance, and you've built a skill that generalizes further than you might expect.

There's a related cost that deserves its own mention: fusion doesn't just distort how you see a single number. It distorts how you see your own trajectory over time. A person permanently fused to their current balance experiences every check-in as a fresh, isolated verdict, disconnected from the six months or six years before it — as if the number arrived from nowhere, unrelated to any pattern, unrelated to the slow, real progress that might actually be underway. Defusion, practiced consistently, does something quietly powerful here: it lets you finally see the number as one point in a sequence rather than a standalone sentence, which means you can start noticing trends instead of just absorbing verdicts. That's a different, better relationship to have with your own financial life — not a courtroom convening fresh every time you look, but a story with a shape, a shape you're finally in a position to actually track.

The overrides

One caution worth naming before the overrides: defusion is a practice, not a switch. The first time you try naming a thought as a thought — "I'm having the thought that I'm failing," rather than simply "I'm failing" — it will feel stilted, almost silly, like a technique rather than a feeling. That's normal, and it doesn't mean it isn't working. The awkwardness is the sound of a new pathway being built where an old, well-worn one used to run automatically. Expect the fusion to still win sometimes, especially under real pressure, especially with the numbers that carry the most history. The measure of progress here isn't a permanent absence of fusion. It's noticing, a little sooner each time, that you're fused — and that noticing, repeated enough times, is what eventually shortens the whole event from a spiral to a flicker.

Speak the number before you feel the number. When you open any account, statement, or bill, say the figure out loud in a flat, literal sentence before you let yourself react — "the balance is X," "the bill is Y," nothing added. This isn't a trick to feel better. It's a half-second delay that lets you catch the fact before the old verdict grabs it, and that half-second is where defusion lives.

The Move: name the thought as a thought. The next time a number produces the familiar heat — shame, dread, the urge to close the tab — say, silently or out loud, "I'm having the thought that this number means I'm failing." Not "I'm failing." "I'm *having the thought* that I'm failing." That extra clause is the entire mechanism: it puts the thought back in your hand as an object you're holding, instead of a truth you're standing inside. Do this once, deliberately, this week, on one real number

— and notice, afterward, that the thought didn't disappear, but you're no longer fused to it. It's an object now. You can set it down.

Write the fact and the feeling in two separate columns. Take one number you've been avoiding. In one column, write only what's verifiably true — the balance, the due date, the interest rate. In the other, write the story your mind attaches to it — what it supposedly says about you. Read the two columns side by side. You'll notice the left column is short and boring. The right column is long and dramatic and, on inspection, entirely unsupported by anything in the left. Seeing them side by side, in your own handwriting, does more to break the fusion than any amount of reasoning with yourself in your head.

Keep the page. Don't throw it away after the exercise. The next time a related number produces the same familiar heat, pull the old page back out before starting a new one, and notice how the right-hand column from last time reads now, with some distance — often it will look almost embarrassingly overstated, dramatic in a way that's easier to see in hindsight than in the moment it was written. That noticing, repeated across several numbers over several months, is itself a form of evidence: proof, in your own handwriting, that the story column has a long history of overstating the case. Eventually, the right-hand column starts to lose credibility before you've even finished writing it, because you've built a track record of watching it exaggerate.

A last thought before the book's close: defusion is the mechanism this final chapter names explicitly, but if you look back across every chapter before it, you'll notice each one was really teaching a version of the same skill from a different angle — naming the flinch in Chapter 2, translating verdict back into sentence in Chapter 3, catching the old recording in Chapter 4, sizing the unknowns in Chapter 5, disclosing the true number in Chapter 6, logging the honest evidence in Chapter 7, building the four-minute bridge in Chapter 8. All eight are variations on the same underlying move: catching the moment a fact tries to become a verdict, and gently, deliberately, keeping the two apart. That's the actual skill this book has been teaching the whole time, under eight different names, in eight different rooms of a financial life. You don't need to master all eight to benefit. You need to recognize the shape once, clearly, and the rest starts to generalize on its own.

The Rule to Remember: A number can describe your account. It was never qualified to describe you.

Before You Go

Before you go, look at the number waiting for you right now — the balance, the invoice, the line on the spreadsheet you've been meaning to open. Notice what happens in your chest before you even see the digits. That flinch, that small brace — that's not about the number. It never was.

If you're reading this in one sitting, cover to cover, notice that you've just spent several hours inside eight different versions of the same fear, told from eight different angles, and that none of it, at any point, actually asked anything financially difficult of you. No budget. No five-year plan. No app to download. That was deliberate. The hardest work in personal finance isn't usually the math. It's the fifteen minutes before the math, the ones this book has spent its entire length trying to make survivable.

You've watched this in yourself for the length of this book. The good-with-money person who wasn't checking, just performing. The verdict reached in childhood, long before any real evidence came in. The family weather that taught you numbers were dangerous before you could add. The scorekeeping with people who were never actually your competitors. The mask, expensive, exhausting, worn to hide a shame no one else could see. The story that explained everything and therefore excused you from looking at anything. The punishment you handed yourself, again and again, for a crime that was really just being human and afraid. And finally, the number that isn't you — the plain, boring fact that a figure on a screen has no opinion about your worth, even when you've spent years certain it did.

If you go back through these chapters again — and you might, in a month, in a year, whenever the flinch resurfaces stronger than usual, because it will, occasionally, no matter how much practice you've put in — you'll probably notice something you missed the first time through. Each chapter's scene will read a little differently once you've lived a few weeks or months on the other side of it, once "look at the number" has become, even partially, a genuine habit instead of an aspiration. The scenes don't change. You do. That's usually how you'll know the practice is actually working — not because the fear disappears, but because you start reading your own old avoidance with something closer to compassion than recognition, the way you might look back at an old photograph of yourself and think, gently, *oh, you were so scared, and you didn't need to be.*

Here is the thesis this whole book has been circling, said straight: the numbers you refuse to look at were never really about the numbers. They were about who you'd have to admit you are if you looked. Not who you are financially — who you are, period. The person who needed help and didn't ask. The person who spent to feel loved. The person who is, in the end, still figuring it out, at an age when you thought you'd have this handled. Looking at the number means looking at that person. So you looked away, and called it forgetfulness, or busyness, or not being a numbers person. It was never any of those. It was self-protection, and it worked — for a while, at a cost you're only now totaling up.

It's worth being honest, here at the end, about what this book has not promised you. It hasn't promised that your numbers are secretly fine, that looking will always reveal good news, that the fear was always disproportionate to the facts. Sometimes it isn't. Sometimes the balance really is low, the debt really is real, and the work ahead really is a long, unglamorous stretch of repair with no shortcut through it. What this book has argued, instead, is narrower and more durable than false comfort: that the repair work — whatever shape it takes for you — can only start once looking stops feeling like a referendum on your worth. Shame doesn't just make the number harder to face. It makes the number harder to *act on*, because a person in the grip of a verdict is busy defending themselves, not solving a problem. Strip the verdict away, and what's left, even in a genuinely hard financial situation, is just a problem — which is a category of thing human beings are very, very good at solving, once they're not simultaneously trying to prove they're not a bad person for having it.

So here is the one practice to carry out of these pages, the thing to do the next time a number appears and your stomach drops: before you react, name what you're afraid the number will say about you. Not the number itself — the sentence behind it. "If I look, I'll find out I'm careless." "If I look, I'll find out

I'm behind." "If I look, I'll find out I'm not who I told people I was." Say the sentence, silently or out loud, and then look at the number anyway. You will find, almost every time, that the number is smaller than the sentence. It always is. A number is a fact with no feelings about you. It doesn't remember what you did with the money. It doesn't think less of you. It just sits there, waiting to be read, the way a thermometer waits to be read — not a judgment on the weather, just a measurement of it.

This is the whole practice: separate the measurement from the meaning you've been assigning it. Do this enough times and the flinch gets smaller. Not gone — smaller. You'll still feel something when you open the account. But it will feel like weather instead of a verdict, information instead of an indictment. That shift is the entire point of everything you've just read.

If you take nothing else from these pages, take this: the specific mechanism doesn't matter nearly as much as the general shape underneath all eight of them. Every chapter in this book described a different costume the same fear wears — self-verification, family scripts, social comparison, impression management, identity-protective reasoning, moral licensing, cognitive fusion. You don't need to remember the names. You need to remember the shape: a fact arrives, your mind rushes to attach a verdict to it before you've consented, and the verdict, not the fact, is what you've spent years avoiding. Once you can see that shape clearly, in any domain, you have something more valuable than any single override in this book — you have the ability to catch the fusion happening, in real time, whatever new form it takes next. Money was just the domain this book happened to use to teach it to you.

One last practical note, because this book would be incomplete without saying it plainly: nothing here replaces an actual conversation with a financial advisor, a credit counselor, or a trusted professional if your numbers point to a real structural problem — a debt load that needs a repayment plan, a retirement gap that needs an actual strategy, a tax situation that needs an expert rather than a chapter in a book about feelings. Defusing the shame is the first step, not the only one. It's the step that makes the rest of the steps possible, because a person who can look without flinching is a person who can finally sit across from a professional, or open a spreadsheet, or make a phone call, without the conversation being secretly about their worth as a human being instead of about the actual math. Get the shame out of the way. Then get the help you need, if you need it, from people whose job is the math — not the meaning.

Notes & Further Reading

The psychological and behavioral-finance concepts referenced throughout this book draw on established, verifiable research. Readers interested in going deeper are pointed toward the original sources and researchers credited in each chapter, rather than toward secondary summaries.

On self-verification and the drive to confirm an existing self-view: Social psychologist William Swann's research on self-verification — the finding that people are motivated to have their existing self-concept confirmed, even when that self-concept is unflattering — underlies the discussion in Chapter 2 of why a stable, if negative, financial self-image can feel safer to protect than an open, unconfirmed question.

On self-discrepancy theory: Psychologist E. Tory Higgins's research on the gap between a person's actual self and their "ought self" — the self they believe they're supposed to be — and his finding that this specific gap produces agitation and shame rather than the gentler sadness of falling short of an "ideal self," underlies the discussion in Chapter 2 of the checkout-line flinch and why it sharpens in the presence of an audience.

On the distinction between shame and guilt: Brené Brown's research distinguishing shame ("I am bad") from guilt ("I did a bad thing"), and her finding that shame depends on secrecy, silence, and judgment while losing power in the presence of empathy, underlies the discussion in Chapter 3 of why checking a balance can feel like standing trial.

On judgment under uncertainty: Daniel Kahneman and Amos Tversky's foundational research on judgment and decision-making under uncertainty, including their documentation of how people can prefer a bounded, unresolved worry over a precise, fixed fact, informs the discussion in Chapter 3 of why an unfinished calculation can feel safer than a completed one.

On social learning and modeling: Psychologist Albert Bandura's research on social learning — the finding that people acquire behavior, and the emotional charge around it, largely by observing others rather than by direct instruction, with modeling strongest when it comes from closely identified figures repeated consistently over time — underlies the discussion in Chapter 4 of how a household's financial "weather" gets transmitted to a child.

On money scripts: The financial-therapy research of Brad Klontz and Ted Klontz on money scripts — largely unconscious beliefs about money absorbed in childhood, often before age seven, that go on to predict adult financial behavior independent of income or education — underlies the discussion in Chapter 4 of inherited silence-and-avoidance patterns and inherited vigilance-and-narration patterns alike.

On social comparison theory: Psychologist Leon Festinger's social comparison theory — the finding that people evaluate themselves by measuring against similar others rather than against any fixed internal standard, and that comparisons against close peers land harder than comparisons against distant strangers — underlies the discussion in Chapter 5 of why a friend's kitchen renovation stings in a way a stranger's mansion never could. The related distinction between upward and downward comparison, developed by researchers building on

Festinger's framework, informs the same chapter's discussion of why attention drifts toward whichever comparison threatens standing rather than whichever one would soothe it.

On the mere exposure effect and shifting reference points: Robert Zajonc's research on the mere exposure effect — the finding that repeated exposure to something increases favorable regard for it — informs the discussion in Chapter 5 of how a peer group's visible spending can quietly recalibrate a person's sense of a normal baseline over time.

On impression management and dramaturgy: Sociologist Erving Goffman's research on impression management and his dramaturgical framework — the front region where a person performs for an audience, the back region where the performance drops, and his concept of "losing face" as the specific, socially witnessed exposure of a maintained self — underlies the discussion in Chapter 6 of why picking up a check can feel more urgent than affording it.

On the status quo bias: The research of Richard Zeckhauser and William Samuelson identifying the status quo bias — the tendency to preserve a current arrangement because change requires a visible, active decision while staying silent requires nothing — informs the discussion in Chapter 6 of why saying yes before checking a number is its own kind of default.

On identity-protective cognition: Legal scholar Dan Kahan's research on identity-protective cognition — the tendency to process factual information in ways that defend an already-held identity rather than in ways that arrive at the most accurate belief, and his finding that stronger analytical skill does not reduce this tendency and can instead make it more sophisticated — underlies the discussion in Chapter 7 of why an unexpected refund gets filed as "luck" rather than as evidence of competence.

On contingencies of self-worth: The research of Jennifer Crocker and Connie Wolfe on contingencies of self-worth — the finding that evidence in a domain a person has staked their self-esteem on gets processed with more emotional intensity and more defensive filtering than evidence elsewhere — informs the same chapter's discussion of why a single bad investment can feel like an attack on identity rather than an ordinary setback.

On stress, coping, and appraisal: Psychologist Richard Lazarus's research distinguishing problem-focused coping, which addresses the source of distress, from emotion-focused coping, which changes how the distress feels without addressing its source, underlies the discussion in Chapter 8 of why a small purchase after a shame spike can deliver real relief without touching the underlying number.

On tunneling under scarcity: The research of behavioral economists Sendhil Mullainathan and Eldar Shafir on scarcity and tunneling — the finding that a mind under real or feared financial strain narrows its attention to the most immediately urgent demand, often at the cost of the slightly-further-out problems that would have eased the pressure — informs the discussion in the opening chapter of why an avoided account so rarely gets the calm, unhurried attention it needs.

On cognitive fusion and defusion: Psychologist Steven Hayes developed Acceptance and Commitment Therapy and its concept of cognitive fusion — the mind's habit of treating a thought as identical to the reality it describes, rather than as one perspective on it that can be examined. That concept, along with the accompanying practice of defusion, underlies the discussion in the book's final chapter of what it means to separate a number from the verdict fused to it.

This book does not cite any statistic, study, or survey not directly attributable to a named researcher or well-established body of research. Where a mechanism is described without a specific citation — moral licensing and guilt-driven spending in Chapter 8, for instance — it reflects a broader, widely-documented pattern in behavioral economics and consumer psychology rather than a single study, and readers are encouraged to consult the primary sources above for the full depth of the underlying research.

This book addresses ordinary, non-clinical shame and avoidance patterns around money — the flinch before checking a balance, the unopened statement, the inherited family silence — and it is not a substitute for professional mental health support. If your relationship to money involves more severe shame, a history of financial trauma or abuse, compulsive spending you cannot interrupt on your own, or shame significant enough to affect your daily functioning or safety, please seek support from a licensed therapist or counselor. This book also is not financial advice. It does not recommend any specific investment, account, platform, debt-repayment strategy, or allocation, and nothing in it should be treated as a substitute for guidance from a qualified financial professional or credit counselor familiar with your specific circumstances. Its subject is behavioral: the psychology of shame and avoidance around looking at your own numbers, not the question of what you should actually do with them once you have.

About

The Shame Instinct is part of a library exploring the wired-in patterns that shape how people relate to money — not as a series of character flaws to overcome through willpower, but as a set of honest, researched mechanisms built into every human nervous system, worth understanding on their own terms. Each book in the library isolates one distinct pattern, traces it to its real psychological roots, and offers concrete, decision-level ways to work with it rather than against it.

Every book in this library is built the same way: one pattern, traced honestly to real research, translated into overrides you can actually use under pressure rather than only in hindsight. None of them promise to remove the pattern they describe. All of them are trying to do the one thing that actually holds up under real conditions — widen the gap between the moment the pattern fires and the moment you act on it, until there's room in that gap for the calmer, more complete version of you to have a say.

None of these books ask you to become a different kind of person. They ask you to notice, honestly and without judgment, which specific pattern tends to run the show when the pressure arrives — and then to build one small, concrete piece of structure around that specific pattern, in advance, while you're calm enough to build it well. That's the entire method, repeated across every pattern this library covers. It isn't dramatic. It doesn't promise transformation. It just quietly works, one widened gap at a time, which turns out to be exactly the kind of unglamorous, durable progress that actually holds up on the days that matter most.

If this book helped you see the number as a number instead of a verdict, even once, the next useful step is simple: open the account you've been avoiding, sooner than you would have before, and notice you're still you on the other side of it. That's the whole practice. It doesn't get more complicated than that, and it doesn't need to.

You were never bad with money. You were a person protecting a self you were afraid to find out the truth about. That person doesn't need to hide anymore. The number was never coming for you. Go look.

Also in the Series

Every book in The Money Instinct library stands on its own — read them in any order. If this one was useful, the library continues:

The Money Instinct

The Secrecy Instinct

The Underearning Instinct

The Panic Instinct

The Merge Instinct

The Ceiling Instinct

The Windfall Instinct

The Control Instinct

The Legacy Instinct

The Comparison Instinct

The Enabling Instinct

The Austerity Instinct

The Paralysis Instinct

The Retirement Instinct

The Divorce Instinct

The Enough Instinct

The Overconfidence Instinct

The Vigilance Instinct

The Generosity Instinct

www.ingramcontent.com/pod-product-compliance
Lightning Source LLC
LaVergne TN
LVHW010718061126
851857LV00014B/1240
* 9 7 8 1 8 0 4 2 8 1 0 0 0 *